A FAMILY
TREASURY OF POETRY

A FAMILY
TREASURY OF POETRY

SELECTED AND INTRODUCED BY NEIL PHILIP

Illustrated by John Lawrence

DORLING KINDERSLEY
LONDON • NEW YORK • SYDNEY • MOSCOW

A DORLING KINDERSLEY BOOK

FOR SAM, JESSICA, SARAH, ROISÍN, SINÉAD AND AISLING
NP

FOR TRISTAN, SOPHIE, LOUIS AND JOSH
JL

First published as *A New Treasury of Poetry* by Blackie and Son Ltd 1990

An Albion Book
Concieved, designed and produced by
The Albion Press Ltd, Spring Hill, Idbury, Oxon OX7 6RU

Designer: Emma Bradford
Copy Editor: Robyn Marsack
Permissions: Nick Wetton
Project Co-ordinator: Elizabeth Wilkes

British Library Cataloguing in Publication Data
A New treasury of poetry
I. Children's poetry in English – Anthologies
I. Philip, Neil *1955* – II. Lawrence, John
821.00809282

ISBN 0 7513 0506 5

Typeset in Linotron Perpetua by Wyvern Typesetting Ltd, Bristol
Printed and bound in Hong Kong by South China Printing Co.

CONTENTS

Neil Philip: Introduction   14

Edward Thomas *Words*   17

A CHILD WENT FORTH

Walt Whitman *'There Was a Child Went Forth'*   20
Traditional *Yankee Doodle*   22
Robert Burns *Grace at Kirkudbright*   22
William Blake *Infant Joy*   22
Robert Herrick *Another Grace for a Child*   22
Sylvia Plath *Morning Song*   23
Ted Hughes *I See a Bear*   24
Traditional *Here comes a Lusty Wooer*   24
Gillian Clarke *Baby-sitting*   25
Robert Graves *The Mirror*   25
Traditional *'Lavender's blue'*   26
Traditional *'I know where I'm going'*   26
Charles Causley *My Young Man's a Cornishman*   27
Robert Graves *Henry and Mary*   27
Delmore Schwartz *I am Cherry Alive*   28
John Skelton *To Mistress Margaret Hussey*   29
Charlotte Mew *The Shade-catchers*   29
R. L. Stevenson *Where Go the Boats?*   30
T. E. Hulme *Above the Dock*   30
Vita Sackville-West *Full Moon*   30
Ted Hughes *Full Moon and Little Frieda*   31
John Crowe Ransom *First Travels of Max*   32
May Swenson *The Centaur*   34
W. B. Yeats *The Collar-bone of a Hare*   35
Gwendolyn Brooks *We Real Cool*   35

Edwin Muir *The Brothers* 36
Edgar Allan Poe *Alone* 36
Charles Causley *Nursery Rhyme of Innocence and Experience* 37
Thomas Hood *'I remember, I remember . . .'* 38
Philip Larkin *I Remember, I Remember* 38
Dylan Thomas *Fern Hill* 40
Louis MacNeice *Soap Suds* 42
R. L. Stevenson *'Sing me a song of a lad that is gone'* 43
Charles Causley *Eden Rock* 44
Louis MacNeice *Apple Blossom* 45

DAYS ARE WHERE WE LIVE

Philip Larkin *Days* 48
George Mackay Brown *Beachcomber* 48
Sir Henry Wotton *The Character of a Happy Life* 49
Edward de Vere, Earl of Oxford *'Were I a king . . .'* 49
Algernon Charles Swinburne *A Child's Laughter* 50
W. B. Yeats *Running to Paradise* 51
Eleanor & Herbert Farjeon *William I* 52
Rudyard Kipling *The Looking Glass* 54
Queen Elizabeth I *'When I was fair and young . . .'* 55
John Wilmot, Earl of Rochester *Impromptu on Charles II* 56
Anon. *On Prince Frederick* 56
Emily Dickinson *'I'm Nobody! Who are you?'* 56
Stevie Smith *The Frog Prince* 57
John Heath-Stubbs *Two Wedding Songs* 58
Robert Graves *Vain and Careless* 60
George Ridley *Cushie Butterfield* 61
Traditional *The Water is Wide* 62
Robert Burns *A Red, Red Rose* 62
Frank Collymore *Ballad of an Old Woman* 63
John Keats *A Song About Myself* 64
Edward Lear *How Pleasant to Know Mr Lear* 66

CONTENTS

T. S. Eliot *Lines for Cuscuscaraway and Mirza Murad Ali Beg* 67
Walt Whitman *From Song of Myself* 67
Walter Savage Landor *On His Seventy-Fifth Birthday* 68
E. C. Bentley *'The Art of Biography'* 68
Roger McGough *Poem for a Dead Poet* 68
Seamus Heaney *Saint Francis and the Birds* 69
Robert Graves *Love without Hope* 70
Ivor Gurney *Walking Song* 70
Charlotte Mew *Afternoon Tea* 71
Traditional *'One leg . .'* 72
Walter Raleigh *Wishes of an Elderly Man* 72
Robert Frost *House Fear* 72
William Carlos Williams *This Is Just to Say* 72
Sonia Sanchez *Poem at Thirty* 73
Frances Cornford *A Recollection* 73
Peter Porter *A Consumer's Report* 74
A. E. Housman *'The laws of God, the laws of man'* 76
Robert Graves *Song: Lift-Boy* 77

BIRDS AND BEASTS

John Heath-Stubbs *The History of the Flood* 80
George Turberville *The Lover Whose Mistress Feared a Mouse,
    Declareth That He Would Become a Cat, If He Might Have His Desire* 84
Christopher Smart *From Jubilate Agno* 85
T. S. Eliot *The Rum Tum Tugger* 87
Oliver Goldsmith *On the Death of a Mad Dog* 89
Edith Sitwell *The Cat* 89
John Clare *Hares at Play* 90
Traditional *The Oyster* 90
W. W. E. Ross *Fish* 90
Elizabeth Bishop *The Fish* 91
Leigh Hunt *Three Sonnets: To a Fish, A Fish replies, The Fish
    turns into a Man, and then into a Spirit, and again speaks* 92

William Wordsworth *To a Butterfly*   94
S. T. Coleridge *Answer to a Child's Question*   94
Robert Graves *Allie*   95
John Clare *Little Trotty Wagtail*   95
Traditional *Robin Redbreast's Testament*   96
Gerard Manley Hopkins *'Repeat that, repeat'*   97
Francis Quarles *On the Cuckoo*   97
Traditional *The Cuckoo*   97
Andrew Young *Wiltshire Downs*   98
Alfred Tennyson *The Eagle*   98
Wilfrid Gibson *The Fowler*   99
Wilfrid Gibson *Michael's Song*   99
Emily Dickinson *'A narrow Fellow in the Grass'*   99
D. H. Lawrence *Snake*   100
D. H. Lawrence *Lizard*   103
Alden Nowlan *The Bull Moose*   104
William Blake *The Tyger*   105
Ted Hughes *The Thought-Fox*   105
Walt Whitman *A Noiseless Patient Spider*   106
Ted Hughes *'Yesterday he was nowhere to be found'*   106
Traditional *Poor Old Horse*   108
W. H. Davies *Sheep*   109
Ruth Dallas *Milking Before Dawn*   109
James Reeves *Cows*   110
Thomas Hardy *The Oxen*   111

SING A SONG OF SEASONS

R. L. Stevenson *Autumn Fires*   114
Christina Rossetti *'Bread and milk for breakfast'*   114
Rudyard Kipling *Cuckoo Song*   114
Emily Dickinson *'Dear March — Come in —'*   115
Charlotte Mew *In the Fields*   116
William Blake *Spring*   116

CONTENTS

Charlotte Mew *The Trees Are Down*   117

Charlotte Mew *Domus Caedet Arborem*   118

Robert Southwell *'The lopped tree in time may grow again'*   118

A. E. Housman *'Loveliest of trees, the cherry now'*   119

William Wordsworth *The Daffodils*   120

Robert Herrick *To Daffodils*   120

John Clare *The Wheat ripening*   121

William Canton *Day-Dreams*   121

Archibald Lampman *Heat*   122

James Berry *Pods Pop and Grin*   123

Philip Larkin *Cut Grass*   123

Emily Dickinson *'Blazing in Gold'*   123

Emily Dickinson *'The Sun and Fog contested'*   124

Traditional *The Rainbow*   124

T. E. Hulme *Autumn*   124

Thomas Hardy *Weathers*   124

John Keats *To Autumn*   125

Vita Sackville-West *Beechwoods at Knole*   126

Allen Curnow *Wild Iron*   127

R. L. Stevenson *Windy Nights*   127

Christina Rossetti *'Who has seen the wind?'*   127

Walter de la Mare *The Storm*   128

David Campbell *Windy Gap*   129

Dorothy Wordsworth *Address to a Child during a
   Boisterous Winter Evening*   130

Dorothy Wordsworth *'O thought I!'*   131

Ivor Gurney *The High Hills*   132

Ted Hughes *'An October robin . . .'*   132

Walter de la Mare *'Please to remember'*   133

Emily Dickinson *'There's a certain Slant of light'*   134

Edward Thomas *Snow*   134

Thomas Campion *Now Winter Nights Enlarge*   135

Robert Frost *Stopping by Woods on a Snowy Evening*   136

Edward Thomas *Thaw*   136

Andrew Young *Sudden Thaw*   137

William Blake *Song by an Old Shepherd*   137

Gillian Hughes *Snow Falling*   138

Traditional *Christmas Song*   139

CHILDREN IF YOU DARE TO THINK

Robert Graves *Warning to Children*   142
W. H. Davies *Leisure*   142
John Keats *'A thing of beauty is a joy for ever'*   143
Edward Thomas *Cock-Crow*   143
W. B. Yeats *The Lake Isle of Innisfree*   144
Elinor Wylie *Prophecy*   144
A. E. Housman *'White in the moon . . .'*   144
Algernon Charles Swinburne *'Before the beginning of years'*   145
e. e. cummings *'i thank You God . . .'*   146
Gerard Manley Hopkins *Pied Beauty*   146
Rudyard Kipling *'Cities and Thrones and Powers'*   147
Percy Bysshe Shelley *Ozymandias*   148
Sir Walter Ralegh *'Even such is Time . . .'*   148
Emily Dickinson *'A word is dead'*   149
William Blake *'He who binds to himself a joy'*   149
James Berry *Fantasy of an African Boy*   149
Laurence Binyon *Hunger*   150
Leigh Hunt *Abou Ben Adhem*   151
John Clare *Song*   152
William Blake *A Poison Tree*   153
Traditional *'Dont-care didn't care'*   153
Stevie Smith *Anger's Freeing Power*   154
Adam McNaughtan *The Jeely Piece Song*   155
Hugh MacDiarmid *The Glog-Hole*   156
Langston Hughes *'I, too, sing America'*   156
Iain Crichton Smith *None is the same as another*   156
Sir Walter Ralegh *As You Came from the Holy Land*   157
W. H. Davies *The Beautiful*   158
Robert Frost *The Road Not Taken*   158
Traditional *This Is the Key*   158
Emily Dickinson *'The Brain — is wider than the Sky —'*   159
Ivor Gurney *Generations*   159
Alfred Tennyson *Merlin and the Gleam*   160
D. H. Lawrence *The Rainbow*   162
Walter de la Mare *The Rainbow*   162
William Wordsworth *'My heart leaps up'*   162
Gerard Manley Hopkins *'The child is father to the man'*   162

Christina Rossetti *'What are heavy?'*   163
Arthur Hugh Clough *'Say not the struggle nought availeth . . .'*   163
Emily Dickinson *'In this short Life'*   164
Langston Hughes *Personal*   164
Arthur Hugh Clough *'Where lies the land . . .'*   164
Charles Causley *I Am the Great Sun*   165
Emily Dickinson *'I took one Draught of Life —'*   165
William Blake *From Auguries of Innocence*   165

ONCE UPON A TIME

Robert Southey *The Cataract of Lodore*   168
Thomas Love Peacock *The War Song of Dinas Vawr*   170
W. H. Auden *Roman Wall Blues*   171
Wilfrid Gibson *The Wishing-Well*   171
Michael Drayton *The Ballad of Agincourt*   172
Rudyard Kipling *A Smuggler's Song*   174
Charles Wolfe *The Burial of Sir John Moore at Corunna*   175
Ivor Gurney *To His Love*   176
Les A. Murray *Morse*   177
Alfred Noyes *The Highwayman*   178
Walter de la Mare *The Listeners*   182
Rudyard Kipling *The Way through the Woods*   183
Denis Glover *The Magpies*   184
Jeremiah John Callanan *The Outlaw of Loch Lene*   185
John Keats *La Belle Dame Sans Merci*   186
A. E. Housman *'Her strong enchantments failing'*   187
Edwin Arlington Robinson *Richard Cory*   187
Traditional *Lord Randal*   188
Traditional *Frankie and Johnny*   189
Traditional *The Douglas Tragedy*   190
Sir Walter Scott *Young Lochinvar*   192
Traditional *Our Ship she lies in Harbour*   194
Matthew Arnold *The Forsaken Merman*   195
Rudyard Kipling *Song of the Galley-Slaves*   199

THE LAND OF WHIPPERGINNY

Robert Graves *The Land of Whipperginny*   202
William Hart-Smith *Boomerang*   202
Louis MacNeice *Invocation*   203
Sir Francis Beaumont *'Shake off your heavy trance'*   204
Andrew Salkey *John Connu Rider*   204
W. B. Yeats *The Song of Wandering Aengus*   205
Traditional *I saw a Peacock*   206
Traditional *'How many miles to Babylon?'*   206
W. J. Turner *Romance*   207
Edgar Allan Poe *Eldorado*   207
Anon. *Loving Mad Tom*   208
Walter de la Mare *Bunches of Grapes*   209
Christina Rossetti *'Three plum buns'*   210
John Keats *Dawlish Fair*   210
Traditional *King Arthur*   210
Edward Blishen *'Amid the derringers I ride'*   211
Traditional *The Yule Days*   212
Judith Wright *Legend*   214
Traditional *The Derby Ram*   216
William Shakespeare *Ariel's Song*   217
Walter de la Mare *The Song of the Mad Prince*   217
Charles Causley *Figgie Hobbin*   218
Edward Lear *Calico Pie*   219
Joan Aiken *How to make a sailor's pie*   220
Traditional *Grey Goose and Gander*   220
Ivor Gurney *Sea-Marge*   220
Christina Rossetti *'Ferry me across the water'*   221
Walter de la Mare *The Silver Penny*   222
Traditional *'I had a little nut-tree'*   222
A. E. Housman *'Into my heart an air that kills'*   222
Edward Lear *The Owl and the Pussy-cat*   223
James Reeves *Spells*   224
James Joyce *'Lean out of the window'*   225
William Blake *'I give you the end of a golden string'*   225

GOODNIGHT

Eleanor Farjeon *Good Night*   228
Traditional *A Lyke-Wake Dirge*   228
W. S. Gilbert *A Nightmare*   229
James Reeves *The Sea*   231
James Reeves *Slowly*   231
Samuel Palmer *Twilight Time*   232
Charles Causley *Samuel Palmer's Coming from Evening Church*   233
William Blake *The Echoing Green*   234
Henry Vaughan *The Morning Watch*   235
John Bunyan *The Shepherd Boy's Song*   236
Eleanor Farjeon *The Tide in the River*   236
Ivor Gurney *The Songs I Had*   236
John Clare *A Vision*   236
John Masefield *Sea-Fever*   237
Christina Rossetti *Up-hill*   238
R. L. Stevenson *Requiem*   238
George Macdonald *A Baby-Sermon*   238
William Morris *Lines for a Bed at Kelmscott Manor*   239
James Reeves *Time to go Home*   240
Harry Stephens *A Night-Herding Song*   241
Dorothy Wordsworth *The Cottager to Her Infant*   242
Anon. *Weep You No More, Sad Fountains*   242
Robert Greene *Sephestia's Song*   243
Theodore Roethke *My Papa's Waltz*   244
Dennis Scott *Grampa*   244
Rudyard Kipling *The City of Sleep*   245
Robert Frost *After Apple-picking*   246
John Clare *Pleasant Sounds*   247
Alastair Reid *A Spell for Sleeping*   248
Traditional *'Matthew, Mark, Luke, and John'*   249
Walt Whitman *A Clear Midnight*   249

Index of Poets   250

Index of Titles and First Lines   251

Acknowledgements   255

INTRODUCTION

Poetry is more a quality of looking and feeling than a set of rules about rhythm and rhyme. Its task is to describe, explore and define the world. Because the world is endless, poetry is endless. Something new is always coming along.

This book is a collection of poems chosen with the young and inexperienced reader in mind. This does not mean they are only suitable for the young and inexperienced. True poetry, from the simplest to the most challenging, never loses its appeal.

I have kept this quality of lasting freshness in mind while making my choice. Newly-encountered poems which appealed to me on first reading had to continue to do so; poems which I remembered with joy from my early reading had to thrill me still. There is no poem in this book which does not make me shiver with pleasure as I read it.

Poems which on repeated readings cause such a shiver are poems with some quality of mystery in them. So there is no poem in this book which I would claim to understand in any complete or final sense. I have an understanding of each poem which changes with each reading.

In some ways poetry is most akin to magic. Every poem is a sort of spell. Samuel Taylor Coleridge's famous definition of poetry could also be a definition of a spell: 'the best words in the best order'. Another definition, W. H. Auden's, is more down-to-earth: 'memorable speech'. Yet another, A. E. Housman's, encompasses my 'shiver': 'Experience has taught me, when I am shaving of a morning, to keep watch over my thoughts, because, if a line of poetry strays into my memory, my skin bristles so that the razor ceases to act. This particular symptom is accompanied by a shiver down the spine.'

Because I have put such an emphasis on poems which last, poems which will travel through life with you, I have been very cautious with modern poems. Today's favourite may be utterly forgotten tomorrow. I have also been cautious with poems written specially for children, preferring on the whole work which makes itself available to a young reader without any sense of talking or writing down.

Of course some poets have written marvellously for children. From William Blake and Christopher Smart through Robert Louis Stevenson and Christina Rossetti, from Walter de la Mare and Eleanor Farjeon to Ted Hughes and Charles Causley, major poets have identified and addressed imaginative qualities in children which chime with their own concerns. Others, such as John Clare, who thought that 'there is nothing but poetry about the existence of childhood', speak with clarity and urgency to the young. Yet others, such as Pope or Dryden, have a much more sophisticated appeal, and fall outside the scope of this anthology. My halting point as a selector was at the very brink of Thomas Hardy. Hardy is not a 'difficult' poet, and he seems to me the greatest English-language poet of the twentieth century, but, a handful of poems apart, his elegiac, retrospective quality makes him an acquired, adult taste. I wanted to choose poems which would have excited or moved me as a child or young adult, and which might do the same for others.

Indeed there are many poems here which I remember clearly from my early reading. Broadly speaking, as its title suggests, it is a selection from and celebration of the central heritage of English verse. There are rich traditions of poetry from which I have plundered only a few pieces. Today's English poetry is an invigorating clamour of voices and dialects. It is not my intention to dismiss or exclude any of those voices, which may be found in other contemporary collections, but simply to offer to readers a selection of poems which appeal to me.

I have limited myself to work in the English language. Translations can be beautiful poems in their own right, and reading poetry in translation can give access to other cultures and visions in a profound and liberating way, but in the end there is a barrier beyond which you can't travel. The journey into a poem in your own language has no end.

In one of the poems in this book, Robert Graves challenges us to 'dare to think'. That is perhaps what poetry is, a special sort of thinking which involves the poet and the reader in an intimate dialogue. In his book *Poetry in the Making*, Ted Hughes defines this sort of thinking:

> There is the inner life, which is the world of final reality, the world of memory, emotion, imagination, intelligence, and natural common sense, and which goes on all the time, consciously or unconsciously, like the heart beat. There is also the thinking process by which we break into that inner life and capture answers and evidence to support the answers out of it. That process of raid, or persuasion, or ambush, or dogged hunting, or surrender, is the kind of thinking we have to learn and if we do not somehow learn it, then our minds lie in us like the fish in the pond of a man who cannot fish.

Poets like Ted Hughes hook their fish with words: words which at their best are, in Ezra Pound's phrase, 'language charged with meaning to the utmost possible degree'.

NEIL PHILIP
Princes Risborough 1989

WORDS

Out of us all
That make rhymes,
Will you choose
Sometimes –
As the winds use
A crack in a wall
Or a drain,
Their joy or their pain
To whistle through –
Choose me,
You English words?

I know you:
You are light as dreams,
Tough as oak,
Precious as gold,
As poppies and corn,
Or an old cloak:
Sweet as our birds
To the ear,
As the burnet rose
In the heat
Of Midsummer:
Strange as the races
Of dead and unborn:
Strange and sweet
Equally,
And familiar,
To the eye,
As the dearest faces
That a man knows,

And as lost homes are:
But though older far
Than oldest yew, –
As our hills are, old, –
Worn new
Again and again;
Young as our streams
After rain:
And as dear
As the earth which you prove
That we love.

Make me content
With some sweetness
From Wales
Whose nightingales
Have no wings, –
From Wiltshire and Kent
And Herefordshire,
And the villages there, –
From the names, and the things
No less.

Let me sometimes dance
With you,
Or climb
Or stand perchance
In ecstasy,
Fixed and free
In a rhyme,
As poets do.

EDWARD THOMAS

A CHILD WENT FORTH

'THERE WAS A CHILD WENT FORTH'

There was a child went forth every day,
And the first object he looked upon and received with wonder or pity or love
    or dread, that object he became,
And that object became part of him for the day or a certain part of the day
    . . . . or for many years or stretching cycles of years.

The early lilacs became part of this child,
And grass, and white and red morning-glories, and white and red clover, and
    the song of the phœbe-bird,
And the March-born lambs, and the sow's pink-faint litter, and the mare's foal,
    and the cow's calf, and the noisy brood of the barnyard or by the mire of
    the pondside .. and the fish suspending themselves so curiously below
    there .. and the beautiful curious liquid .. and the water-plants with their
    graceful flat heads .. all became part of him.

And the field-sprouts of April and May became part of him . . . . wintergrain sprouts,
    and those of the light-yellow corn, and of the esculent roots of the garden,
And the appletrees covered with blossoms, and the fruit afterward . . . . and
    woodberries .. and the commonest weeds by the road;
And the old drunkard staggering home from the outhouse of the tavern whence
    he had lately risen,
And the schoolmistress that passed on her way to the school .. and the friendly
    boys that passed .. and the quarrelsome boys .. and the tidy and
    freshcheeked girls .. and the barefoot Negro boy and girl,
And all the changes of city and country wherever he went.

His own parents .. he that had propelled the fatherstuff at night, and fathered
    him .. and she that conceived him in her womb and birthed him . . . .
    they gave this child more of themselves than that,
They gave him afterward every day . . . . they and of them became part of him.

The mother at home quietly placing the dishes on the suppertable,
The mother with mild words . . . . clean her cap and gown . . . . a wholesome
    odor falling off her person and clothes as she walks by:
The father, strong, selfsufficient, manly, mean, angered, unjust,
The blow, the quick loud word, the tight bargain, the crafty lure,
The family usages, the language, the company, the furniture . . . . the yearning
    and swelling heart,
Affection that will not be gainsayed . . . . The sense of what is real . . . . the
    thought if after all it should prove unreal,
The doubts of daytime and the doubts of nighttime . . . the curious whether and how,
Whether that which appears so is so . . . . Or is it all flashes and specks?
Men and women crowding fast in the streets . . if they are not flashes and
    specks what are they?
The streets themselves, and the facades of houses . . . . the goods in the
    windows,
Vehicles . . teams . . the tiered wharves, and the huge crossing at the ferries;

The village on the highland seen from afar at sunset . . . . the river between,
Shadows . . aureola and mist . . light falling on roofs and gables of white or
    brown, three miles off,
The schooner near by sleepily dropping down the tide . . the little boat
    slacktowed astern,
The hurrying tumbling waves and quickbroken crests and slapping;
The strata of colored clouds . . . . the long bar of maroontint away solitary by
    itself . . . . the spread of purity it lies motionless in,
The horizon's edge, the flying seacrow, the fragrance of saltmarsh and
    shoremud;
These became part of that child who went forth every day, and who now goes
    and will always go forth every day,
And these become of him or her that peruses them now.

WALT WHITMAN

YANKEE DOODLE

Yankee Doodle went to town,
He rode a little pony,
He stuck a feather in his hat
And called it macaroni.
    Yankee Doodle fa, so, la,
    Yankee Doodle dandy.
    Yankee Doodle fa, so, la,
    Buttermilk and brandy.

Yankee Doodle went to town
To buy a pair of trousers,
He swore he could not see the town
For so many houses.
    Yankee Doodle fa, so, la,
    Yankee Doodle dandy.
    Yankee Doodle fa, so, la,
    Buttermilk and brandy.

TRADITIONAL

GRACE AT KIRKUDBRIGHT

Some have meat and cannot eat,
Some cannot eat that want it:
But we have meat and we can eat,
Sae let the Lord be thankit.

ROBERT BURNS

INFANT JOY

'I have no name:
'I am but two days old.'
What shall I call thee?
'I happy am,
'Joy is my name.'
Sweet joy befall thee!

Pretty joy!
Sweet joy but two days old,
Sweet joy I call thee:
Thou dost smile,
I sing the while,
Sweet joy befall thee!

WILLIAM BLAKE

ANOTHER GRACE FOR A CHILD

Here a little child I stand,
Heaving up my either hand;
Cold as Paddocks though they be,
Here I lift them up to Thee,
For a Benizon to fall
On our meat, and on us all. *Amen.*

ROBERT HERRICK

Paddocks: toads

MORNING SONG

Love set you going like a fat gold watch.
The midwife slapped your footsoles, and your bald cry
Took its place among the elements.

Our voices echo, magnifying your arrival. New statue.
In a drafty museum, your nakedness
Shadows our safety. We stand round blankly as walls.

I'm no more your mother
Than the cloud that distils a mirror to reflect its own slow
Effacement at the wind's hand.

All night your moth-breath
Flickers among the flat pink roses. I wake to listen:
A far sea moves in my ear.

One cry, and I stumble from bed, cow-heavy and floral
In my Victorian nightgown.
Your mouth opens clean as a cat's. The window square

Whitens and swallows its dull stars. And now you try
Your handful of notes;
The clear vowels rise like balloons.

SYLVIA PLATH

I SEE A BEAR

I see a bear
Growing out of a bulb in wet soil licks its black tip
With a pink tongue its little eyes
Open and see a present an enormous bulging mystery package
Over which it walks sniffing at seams
Digging at the wrapping overjoyed holding the joy off sniffing and scratching
Teasing itself with scrapings and lickings and the thought of it
And little sips of the ecstasy of it

O bear do not open your package
Sit on your backside and sunburn your belly
It is all there it has actually arrived
No matter how long you dawdle it cannot get away
Shamble about lazily laze there in the admiration of it
With all the insects it's attracted all going crazy
And those others the squirrel with its pop-eyed amazement
The deer with its pop-eyed incredulity
The weasel pop-eyed with envy and trickery
All going mad for a share wave them off laze
Yawn and grin let your heart thump happily
Warm your shining cheek fur in the morning sun

You have got it everything for nothing

TED HUGHES

HERE COMES A LUSTY WOOER

Here comes a lusty wooer,
My a dildin, my a daldin;
Here comes a lusty wooer,
Lily bright and shine a'.

Pray who do you woo?
My a dildin, my a daldin;
Pray who do you woo?
Lily bright and shine a'.

For your fairest daughter,
My a dildin, my a daldin;
For your fairest daughter,
Lily bright and shine a'.

Then there she is for you,
My a dildin, my a daldin;
Then there she is for you,
Lily bright and shine a'.

TRADITIONAL

BABY-SITTING

I am sitting in a strange room listening
For the wrong baby. I don't love
This baby. She is sleeping a snuffly
Roseate, bubbling sleep; she is fair;
She is a perfectly acceptable child.
I am afraid of her. If she wakes
She will hate me. She will shout
Her hot, midnight rage, her nose
Will stream disgustingly and the perfume
Of her breath will fail to enchant me.

To her I will represent absolute
Abandonment. For her it will be worse
Than for the lover cold in lonely
Sheets; worse than for the woman who waits
A moment to collect her dignity
Beside the bleached bone in the terminal ward.
As she rises sobbing from the monstrous land
Stretching for milk-familiar comforting,
She will find me and between us two
It will not come. It will not come.

GILLIAN CLARKE

THE MIRROR

Mirror mirror tell me
Am I pretty or plain?
Or am I downright ugly,
And ugly to remain?

Shall I marry a gentleman?
Shall I marry a clown?
Or shall I marry
Old Knives and Scissors
Shouting through the town?

ROBERT GRAVES

'LAVENDER'S BLUE'

Lavender's blue, dilly dilly: lavender's green;
When I am King, dilly dilly, you shall be Queen.
Who told you that, dilly dilly, who told you so?
'Twas my own heart, dilly dilly, that told me so.

Call up your men, dilly dilly, set them to work;
Some to the plough, dilly dilly, some to the cart;
Some to make hay, dilly dilly, some to thresh corn,
While you and I, dilly dilly, keep ourselves warm.

If I should die, dilly dilly, as well may hap,
Bury me deep, dilly dilly, under the tap;
Under the tap, dilly dilly, I'll tell you why,
That I may drink, dilly dilly, when I am dry.

TRADITIONAL

'I KNOW WHERE I'M GOING'

I know where I'm going,
And I know who's going with me.
I know who I love,
But the dear knows who I'll marry.

I'll have stockings of silk,
Shoes of fine green leather,
Combs to buckle my hair
And a ring for every finger.

Feather beds are soft,
Painted rooms are bonny:
But I'd leave them all
To go with my love Johnny.

Some say he's dark,
But I say he's bonny,
He's the flower of them all,
My handsome, winsome Johnny.

I know where I'm going,
And I know who's going with me.
I know who I love,
But the dear knows who I'll marry.

TRADITIONAL

MY YOUNG MAN'S A CORNISHMAN

My young man's a Cornishman
He lives in Camborne town,
I met him going up the hill
As I was coming down.

His eye is bright as Dolcoath tin,
His body as china clay,
His hair is dark as Werrington Wood
Upon St Thomas's Day.

He plays the rugby football game
On Saturday afternoon,
And we shall walk on Wilsey Down
Under the bouncing moon.

My young man's a Cornishman,
Won't leave me in the lurch,
And one day we shall married be
Up to Trura church.

He's bought me a ring of Cornish gold,
A belt of copper made,
At Bodmin Fair for my wedding-dress
A purse of silver paid.

And I shall give him scalded cream
And starry-gazy pie,
And make him a saffron cake for tea
And a pasty for by and by.

My young man's a Cornishman,
A proper young man is he,
And a Cornish man with a Cornish maid
Is how it belongs to be.

CHARLES CAUSLEY

*A starry-gaze pie is a fish pie, made of pilchards or sardines.
The fish are cooked whole, with the heads piercing the
crust as though gazing up to the heavens.*

Trura church: Truro Cathedral

HENRY AND MARY

Henry was a young king,
  Mary was his queen;
He gave her a snowdrop
  On a stalk of green.

Then all for his kindness
  And all for his care
She gave him a new-laid egg
  In the garden there.

'Love, can you sing?'
          'I cannot sing.'
'Or tell a tale?'
         'Not one I know.'
'Then let us play at queen and king
  As down the garden walks we go.'

ROBERT GRAVES

I AM CHERRY ALIVE

'I am cherry alive,' the little girl sang,
'Each morning I am something new:
I am apple, I am plum, I am just as excited
As the boys who made the Hallowe'en bang:
I am tree, I am cat, I am blossom too:
When I like, if I like, I can be someone new,
Someone very old, a witch in a zoo:
I can be someone else whenever I think who,
And I want to be everything sometimes too:
And the peach has a pit and I know that too,
And I put it in along with everything
To make the grown-ups laugh whenever I sing:
And I sing: *It is true; It is untrue;*
I know, I know, the true is untrue,
The peach has a pit,
The pit has a peach:
And both may be wrong
When I sing my song,
But I don't tell the grown-ups: because it is sad,
And I want them to laugh just like I do
Because they grew up
And forgot what they knew
And they are sure
I will forget it some day too.
They are wrong. They are wrong.
When I sang my song, I knew, I knew!
I am red, I am gold,
I am green, I am blue,
I will always be me,
I will always be new!'

DELMORE SCHWARTZ

TO MISTRESS MARGARET HUSSEY

Merry Margaret
  As midsummer flower,
Gentle as falcon
  Or hawk of the tower:
With solace and gladness,
Much mirth and no madness,
All good and no badness;
  So joyously,
  So maidenly,
  So womanly
  Her demeaning
  In every thing.
  Far, far passing
  That I can indite,
  Or suffice to write
Of Merry Margaret
As midsummer flower,

Gentle as falcon
Or hawk of the tower.
As patient and still
And as full of good will
As fair Isaphill,
Coliander,
Sweet pomander,
Good Cassander;
Steadfast of thought,
Well made, well wrought,
Far may be sought,
Ere that ye can find
So courteous, so kind
As merry Margaret,
This midsummer flower,
Gentle as falcon,
Or hawk of the tower.

JOHN SKELTON

THE SHADE-CATCHERS

I think they were about as high
As haycocks are. They went running by
Catching bits of shade in the sunny street:
'I've got one,' cried sister to brother,
  'I've got two.' 'Now I've got another.'
But scudding away on their little bare feet,
They left the shade in the sunny street.

CHARLOTTE MEW

WHERE GO THE BOATS?

Dark brown is the river,
    Golden is the sand.
It flows along for ever,
    With trees on either hand.

Green leaves a-floating,
    Castles of the foam,
Boats of mine a-boating –
    Where will all come home?

On goes the river
    And out past the mill,
Away down the valley,
    Away down the hill.

Away down the river,
    A hundred miles or more,
Other little children
    Shall bring my boats ashore.

R. L. STEVENSON

ABOVE THE DOCK

Above the quiet dock in midnight,
Tangled in the tall mast's corded height,
Hangs the moon. What seemed so far away
Is but a child's balloon, forgotten after play.

T. E. HULME

FULL MOON

She was wearing the coral taffeta trousers
Someone had brought her from Isfahan,
And the little gold coat with pomegranate blossoms,
And the coral-hafted feather fan;
But she ran down a Kentish lane in the moonlight,
And skipped in the pool of the moon as she ran.

She cared not a rap for all the big planets,
For Betelgeuse or Aldebaran,
And all the big planets cared nothing for her,
That small impertinent charlatan,
As she climbed on a Kentish stile in the moonlight,
And laughed at the sky through the sticks of her fan.

VITA SACKVILLE-WEST

FULL MOON AND LITTLE FRIEDA

A cool small evening shrunk to a dog bark and the clank of a bucket –

And you listening.
A spider's web, tense for the dew's touch.
A pail lifted, still and brimming – mirror
To tempt a first star to a tremor.

Cows are going home in the lane there, looping the hedges with their warm
      wreaths of breath –
A dark river of blood, many boulders,
Balancing unspilled milk.

'Moon!' you cry suddenly, 'Moon! Moon!'

The moon has stepped back like an artist gazing amazed at a work

That points at him amazed.

TED HUGHES

FIRST TRAVELS OF MAX

In that old house of many generations
The best of the Van Vroomans was the youngest.
But even Max, in a chevroned sailor's blouse
And tawny curls far from subdued to the cap,
Had slapped old Katie and removed himself
From games for children; that was because they told
Him never never to set a naughty foot
Into Fool's Forest, where the devil dwelt.

'Become Saint Michael's sword!' said Max to the stick,
And to the stone, 'Be a forty-four revolver!'
Then Max was glad that he had armed so wisely
As darker grew the wood, and shrill with silence.
All good fairies were helpless here; at night
Whipped in an inch of their lives; weeping, forbidden
To play with strange scared truant little boys
Who didn't belong there. Snakes were allowed there
And lizards and adders – people of age and evil
That lay on their bellies and whispered – no bird nor rabbit.
There were more rotten trees than there were sound ones.
In that wood timber was degenerate
And rotted almost faster than it grew.
There were no flowers nor apples. Too much age.
The only innocent thing was really Max,
And even he had beat his little sisters.

The black tarn rose up almost in his face.
It was as black and sudden as the pit
The Adversary digs in the bowels of the earth;
Bubbles were on it, breath of the black beast
(Formed like a spider, white bag for entrails)
Who took that sort of blackness to inhabit
And dangle after bad men in Fool's Forest.
'Must they be bad?' said casuistical Max.
'Mightn't a good boy who stopped saying his prayers
Be allowed to slip into the spider's fingers?'

Max raised his sword – but what can swords do
Against the Prince of the Dark? Max sheathed his point
And crept around the pool.

There in the middle of the wood was the Red Witch.
Max half expected her. He never imagined
A witch's house that would be red and dirty,
Or a witch's bosom wide and yellow as butter,
Or one that combed so many obscene things
From her black hair into her scarlet lap;
He never believed there would attempt to sing
The one that taught the rats to squeal and Bashan's
Bull to bellow.

'Littlest and last Van Vrooman, do you come too?'
She knew him, it appeared, would know him better,
The scarlet hulk of hell with a fat bosom
Pirouetting at the bottom of the forest.
Certainly Max had come, but he was going;
Unequal contests never being commanded
On young knights only armed in innocence.
'When I am a grown man I will come here
And cut your head off!' That was very well.
And no true heart beating in Christendom
Could have said more, but that for the present would do.

Max went straight home, and nothing chilled him more
Than the company kept him by the witch's laugh
And the witch's song, and the creeping of his flesh.

Max is more firmly domiciliated.
A great house is Van Vrooman, a green slope
South to the sun do the great ones inhabit,
And a few children play on the lawn with the nurse.
Max has returned to his play, and you may find him,
His famous curls unsmoothed, if you will call
Where the Van Vroomans live; the tribe Van Vrooman
Live there at least when any are at home.

JOHN CROWE RANSOM

THE CENTAUR

The summer that I was ten –
Can it be there was only one
summer that I was ten? It must

have been a long one then –
each day I'd go out to choose
a fresh horse from my stable

which was a willow grove
down by the old canal.
I'd go on my two bare feet.

But when, with my brother's jack-knife,
I had cut me a long limber horse
with a good thick knob for a head,

and peeled him slick and clean
except a few leaves for the tail,
and cinched my brother's belt

around his head for a rein,
I'd straddle and canter him fast
up the grass bank to the path,

trot along in the lovely dust
that talcumed over his hoofs,
hiding my toes, and turning

his feet to swift half-moons.
The willow knob with the strap
jouncing between my thighs

was the pommel and yet the poll
of my nickering pony's head.
My head and my neck were mine,

yet they were shaped like a horse.
My hair flopped to the side
like the mane of a horse in the wind.

My forelock swung in my eyes,
my neck arched and I snorted.
I shied and skittered and reared,

stopped and raised my knees,
pawed at the ground and quivered.
My teeth bared as we wheeled

and swished through the dust again.
I was the horse and the rider,
and the leather I slapped to his rump

spanked my own behind.
Doubled, my two hoofs beat
a gallop along the bank,

the wind twanged in my mane,
my mouth squared to the bit.
And yet I sat on my steed

quiet, negligent riding,
my toes standing the stirrups,
my thighs hugging his ribs.

At a walk we drew up to the porch.
I tethered him to a paling.
Dismounting, I smoothed my skirt

and entered the dusky hall.
My feet on the clean linoleum
left ghostly toes in the hall.

Where have you been? said my mother.
Been riding. I said from the sink,
and filled me a glass of water.

What's that in your pocket? she said.
Just my knife. It weighted my pocket
and stretched my dress awry.

Go tie back your hair, said my mother,
and *Why is your mouth all green?*
Rob Roy, he pulled some clover
as we crossed the field, I told her.

MAY SWENSON

THE COLLAR-BONE OF A HARE

Would I could cast a sail on the water
Where many a king has gone
And many a king's daughter
And alight at the comely trees and the lawn,
The playing upon pipes and the dancing,
And learn that the best thing is
To change my loves while dancing
And pay but a kiss for a kiss.

I would find by the edge of that water
The collar-bone of a hare
Worn thin by the lapping of water,
And pierce it through with a gimlet, and stare
At the old bitter world where they marry in churches,
And laugh over the untroubled water
At all who marry in churches,
Through the white thin bone of a hare.

W. B. YEATS

WE REAL COOL

The Pool Players.
Seven at the Golden Shovel.

We real cool. We
Left school. We

Lurk late. We
Strike straight. We

Sing sin. We
Thin gin. We

Jazz June. We
Die soon.

GWENDOLYN BROOKS

THE BROTHERS

Last night I watched my brothers play,
The gentle and the reckless one,
In a field two yards away.
For half a century they were gone
Beyond the other side of care
To be among the peaceful dead.
Even in a dream how could I dare
Interrogate that happiness
So wildly spent yet never less?
For still they raced about the green
And were like two revolving suns;
A brightness poured from head to head,
So strong I could not see their eyes
Or look into their paradise.
What were they doing, the happy ones?
Yet where I was they once had been.

I thought, How could I be so dull,
Twenty thousand days ago,
Not to see they were beautiful?
I asked them, Were you really so
As you are now, that other day?
And the dream was soon away.

For then we played for victory
And not to make each other glad.
A darkness covered every head,
Frowns twisted the original face,
And through that mask we could not see
The beauty and the buried grace.

I have observed in foolish awe
The dateless mid-days of the law
And seen indifferent justice done
By everyone on everyone.
And in a vision I have seen
My brothers playing on the green.

EDWIN MUIR

ALONE

From childhood's hour I have not been
As others were, – I have not seen
As others saw, – I could not bring
My passions from a common spring.
From the same source I have not taken
My sorrow; I could not awaken
My heart to joy at the same tone;
And all I loved, *I* loved alone.
Then – in my childhood – in the dawn
Of a most stormy life was drawn
From every depth of good and ill
The mystery which binds me still:
From the torrent, or the fountain,
From the red cliff of the mountain,
From the sun that round me rolled
In its autumn tint of gold, –
From the lightning in the sky
As it passed me flying by, –
From the thunder and the storm,

And the cloud that took the form
(When the rest of Heaven was blue)
Of a demon in my view.

· EDGAR ALLAN POE

NURSERY RHYME
OF
INNOCENCE AND EXPERIENCE

I had a silver penny
　　And an apricot tree
And I said to the sailor
　　On the white quay

'Sailor O sailor
　　Will you bring me
If I give you my penny
　　And my apricot tree

'A fez from Algeria
　　An Arab drum to beat
A little gilt sword
　　And a parakeet?'

And he smiled and he kissed me
　　As strong as death
And I saw his red tongue
　　And I felt his sweet breath

'You may keep your penny
　　And your apricot tree
And I'll bring your presents
　　Back from sea.'

O the ship dipped down
　　On the rim of the sky
And I waited while three
　　Long summers went by

Then one steel morning
　　On the white quay
I saw a grey ship
　　Come in from sea

Slowly she came
　　Across the bay
For her flashing rigging
　　Was shot away

All round her wake
　　The seabirds cried
And flew in and out
　　Of the hole in her side

Slowly she came
　　In the path of the sun
And I heard the sound
　　Of a distant gun

And a stranger came running
　　Up to me
From the deck of the ship
　　And he said, said he

'O are you the boy
　　Who would wait on the quay
With the silver penny
　　And the apricot tree?

'I've a plum-coloured fez
　　And a drum for thee
And a sword and a parakeet
　　From over the sea.'

'O where is the sailor
　　With bold red hair?
And what is that volley
　　On the bright air?

'O where are the other
　　Girls and boys?
And why have you brought me
　　Children's toys?'

CHARLES CAUSLEY

'I REMEMBER, I REMEMBER . . .'

I remember, I remember
The house where I was born,
The little window where the sun
Came peeping in at morn;
He never came a wink too soon
Nor brought too long a day;
But now, I often wish the night
Had borne my breath away.

I remember, I remember
The roses, red and white,
The violets, and the lily-cups –
Those flowers made of light!
The lilacs where the robin built,
And where my brother set
The laburnum on his birthday, –
The tree is living yet!

I remember, I remember
Where I was used to swing,
And thought the air must rush as fresh
To swallows on the wing;
My spirit flew in feathers then
That is so heavy now,
And summer pools could hardly cool
The fever on my brow.

I remember, I remember
The fir trees dark and high;
I used to think their slender tops
Were close against the sky:
It was a childish ignorance,
But now 'tis little joy
To know I'm farther off from Heaven
Than when I was a boy.

THOMAS HOOD

I REMEMBER, I REMEMBER

Coming up England by a different line
For once, early in the cold new year,
We stopped, and, watching men with number-plates
Sprint down the platform to familiar gates,
'Why, Coventry!' I exclaimed. 'I was born here.'

I leant far out, and squinnied for a sign
That this was still the town that had been 'mine'
So long, but found I wasn't even clear
Which side was which. From where those cycle-crates
Were standing, had we annually departed

For all those family hols? . . . A whistle went:
Things moved. I sat back, staring at my boots.
'Was that,' my friend smiled, 'where you "have your roots"?'
No, only where my childhood was unspent,
I wanted to retort, just where I started:

By now I've got the whole place clearly charted.
Our garden, first: where I did not invent
Blinding theologies of flowers and fruits,
And wasn't spoken to by an old hat.
And here we have that splendid family

I never ran to when I got depressed,
The boys all biceps and the girls all chest,
Their comic Ford, their farm where I could be
'Really myself'. I'll show you, come to that,
The bracken where I never trembling sat,

Determined to go through with it; where she
Lay back, and 'all became a burning mist'.
And, in those offices, my doggerel
Was not set up in blunt ten-point, nor read
By a distinguished cousin of the mayor,

Who didn't call and tell my father *There
Before us, had we the gift to see ahead* –
'You look as if you wished the place in Hell,'
My friend said, 'judging from your face.' 'Oh well,
I suppose it's not the place's fault,' I said.

'Nothing, like something, happens anywhere.'

PHILIP LARKIN

FERN HILL

Now as I was young and easy under the apple boughs
About the lilting house and happy as the grass was green,
   The night above the dingle starry,
     Time let me hail and climb
   Golden in the heydays of his eyes,
And honoured among wagons I was prince of the apple towns
And once below a time I lordly had the trees and leaves
     Trail with daisies and barley
   Down the rivers of the windfall light.

And as I was green and carefree, famous among the barns
About the happy yard and singing as the farm was home,
   In the sun that is young once only,
     Time let me play and be
   Golden in the mercy of his means,
And green and golden I was huntsman and herdsman, the calves
Sang to my horn, the foxes on the hills barked clear and cold,
     And the sabbath rang slowly
   In the pebbles of the holy streams.

All the sun long it was running, it was lovely, the hay
Fields high as the house, the tunes from the chimneys, it was air
   And playing, lovely and watery
     And fire green as grass.
   And nightly under the simple stars
As I rode to sleep the owls were bearing the farm away,
All the moon long I heard, blessed among stables, the nightjars
   Flying with the ricks, and the horses
     Flashing into the dark.

And then to awake, and the farm, like a wanderer white
With the dew, come back, the cock on his shoulder: it was all
   Shining, it was Adam and maiden,
     The sky gathered again
   And the sun grew round that very day.
So it must have been after the birth of the simple light
In the first, spinning place, the spellbound horses walking warm
   Out of the whinnying green stable
     On to the fields of praise.

And honoured among foxes and pheasants by the gay house
Under the new made clouds and happy as the heart was long,
   In the sun born over and over,
     I ran my heedless ways,
   My wishes raced through the house high hay
And nothing I cared, at my sky blue trades, that time allows
In all his tuneful turning so few and such morning songs
   Before the children green and golden
     Follow him out of grace,

Nothing I cared, in the lamb white days, that time would take me
Up to the swallow thronged loft by the shadow of my hand,
   In the moon that is always rising,
     Nor that riding to sleep
   I should hear him fly with the high fields
And wake to the farm forever fled from the childless land.
Oh as I was young and easy in the mercy of his means,
     Time held me green and dying
   Though I sang in my chains like the sea.

      DYLAN THOMAS

SOAP SUDS

This brand of soap has the same smell as once in the big
House he visited when he was eight: the walls of the bathroom open
To reveal a lawn where a great yellow ball rolls back through a hoop
To rest at the head of a mallet held in the hands of a child.

And these were the joys of that house: a tower with a telescope;
Two great faded globes, one of the earth, one of the stars;
A stuffed black dog in the hall; a walled garden with bees;
A rabbit warren; a rockery; a vine under glass; the sea.

To which he has now returned. The day of course is fine
And a grown-up voice cries Play! The mallet slowly swings,
Then crack, a great gong booms from the dog-dark hall and the ball
Skims forward through the hoop and then through the next and then

Through hoops where no hoops were and each dissolves in turn
And the grass has grown head-high and an angry voice cries Play!
But the ball is lost and the mallet slipped long since from the hands
Under the running tap that are not the hands of a child.

LOUIS MACNEICE

'SING ME A SONG OF A LAD THAT IS GONE'

Sing me a song of a lad that is gone,
  Say, could that lad be I?
Merry of soul he sailed on a day
  Over the sea to Skye.

Mull was astern, Rhum on the port,
  Eigg on the starboard bow;
Glory of youth glowed in his soul:
  Where is that glory now?

Sing me a song of a lad that is gone,
  Say, could that lad be I?
Merry of soul he sailed on a day
  Over the sea to Skye.

Give me again all that was there,
  Give me the sun that shone!
Give me the eyes, give me the soul,
  Give me the lad that's gone!

Sing me a song of a lad that is gone,
  Say, could that lad be I?
Merry of soul he sailed on a day
  Over the sea to Skye.

Billow and breeze, islands and seas,
  Mountains of rain and sun,
All that was good, all that was fair,
  All that was me is gone.

R. L. STEVENSON

EDEN ROCK

They are waiting for me somewhere beyond Eden Rock:
My father, twenty-five, in the same suit
Of Genuine Irish Tweed, his terrier Jack
Still two years old and trembling at his feet.

My mother, twenty-three, in a sprigged dress
Drawn at the waist, ribbon in her straw hat,
Has spread the stiff white cloth over the grass.
Her hair, the colour of wheat, takes on the light.

She pours tea from a Thermos, the milk straight
From an old H.P. sauce-bottle, a screw
Of paper for a cork; slowly sets out
The same three plates, the tin cups painted blue.

The sky whitens as if lit by three suns.
My mother shades her eyes and looks my way
Over the drifted stream. My father spins
A stone along the water. Leisurely,

They beckon to me from the other bank.
I hear them call, 'See where the stream-path is!
Crossing is not as hard as you might think.'

I had not thought that it would be like this.

CHARLES CAUSLEY

APPLE BLOSSOM

The first blossom was the best blossom
For the child who never had seen an orchard;
For the youth whom whisky had led astray
The morning after was the first day.

The first apple was the best apple
For Adam before he heard the sentence;
When the flaming sword endorsed the Fall
The trees were his to plant for all.

The first ocean was the best ocean
For the child from streets of doubt and litter;
For the youth for whom the skies unfurled
His first love was his first world.

But the first verdict seemed the worst verdict
When Adam and Eve were expelled from Eden;
Yet when the bitter gates clanged to
The sky beyond was just as blue.

For the next ocean is the first ocean
And the last ocean is the first ocean
And, however often the sun may rise,
A new thing dawns upon our eyes.

For the last blossom is the first blossom
And the first blossom is the best blossom
And when from Eden we take our way
The morning after is the first day.

LOUIS MACNEICE

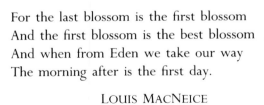

DAYS ARE WHERE WE LIVE

BEACHCOMBER

Monday I found a boot –
Rust and salt leather.
I gave it back to the sea, to dance in.

Tuesday a spar of timber worth thirty bob.
Next winter
It will be a chair, a coffin, a bed.

Wednesday a half can of Swedish spirits.
I tilted my head.
The shore was cold with mermaids and angels.

Thursday I got nothing, seaweed,
A whale bone,
Wet feet and a loud cough.

Friday I held a seaman's skull,
Sand spilling from it
The way time is told on kirkyard stones.

Saturday a barrel of sodden oranges.
A Spanish ship
Was wrecked last month at The Kame.

Sunday for fear of the elders,
I sit on my bum.
What's heaven? A sea chest with
  a thousand gold coins.

GEORGE MACKAY BROWN

kirkyard: churchyard
the elders: of the church

DAYS

What are days for?
Days are where we live.
They come, they wake us
Time and time over.
They are to be happy in:
Where can we live but days?

Ah, solving that question
Brings the priest and the doctor
In their long coats
Running over the fields.

PHILIP LARKIN

THE CHARACTER OF A HAPPY LIFE

How happy is he born and taught
  That serveth not another's will;
Whose armour is his honest thought,
  And simple truth his utmost skill;

Whose passions not his masters are;
  Whose soul is still prepar'd for death,
Untied unto the world by care
  Of public fame or private breath;

Who envies none that chance doth raise,
  Nor vice; who never understood
How deepest wounds are given by praise;
  Nor rules of state, but rules of good;

Who hath his life from rumours freed,
  Whose conscience is his strong retreat;
Whose state can neither flatterers feed,
  Nor ruin make accusers great;

Who God doth late and early pray
  More of His grace than gifts to lend;
And entertains the harmless day
  With a well-chosen book or friend;

This man is freed from servile bands
  Of hope to rise, or fear to fall;
Lord of himself, though not of lands;
  And having nothing, yet hath all.

SIR HENRY WOTTON

'WERE I A KING . . .'

Were I a king I could command content.
  Were I obscure, hidden should be my cares.
Or were I dead, no cares should me torment,
  Nor hopes, nor hates, nor loves, nor griefs, nor fears,
A doubtful choice, of these three which to crave,
A kingdom, or a cottage, or a grave.

EDWARD DE VERE, EARL OF OXFORD

A CHILD'S LAUGHTER

All the bells of heaven may ring,
All the birds of heaven may sing,
All the wells on earth may spring,
All the winds on earth may bring
   All sweet sounds together;
Sweeter far than all things heard,
Hand of harper, tone of bird,
Sound of woods at sundawn stirred,
Welling water's winsome word,
   Wind in warm wan weather,

One thing yet there is, that none
Hearing ere its chime be done
Knows not well the sweetest one
Heard of man beneath the sun,
   Hoped in heaven hereafter;
Soft and strong and loud and light,
Very sound of very light
Heard from morning's rosiest height,
When the soul of all delight
   Fills a child's clear laughter.

Golden bells of welcome rolled
Never forth such notes, nor told
Hours so blithe in tones so bold,
As the radiant mouth of gold
   Here that rings forth heaven.
If the golden-crested wren
Were a nightingale – why, then,
Something seen and heard of men
Might be half as sweet as when
   Laughs a child of seven.

ALGERNON CHARLES SWINBURNE

RUNNING TO PARADISE

As I came over Windy Gap
They threw a halfpenny into my cap,
For I am running to Paradise;
And all that I need do is to wish
And somebody puts his hand in the dish
To throw me a bit of salted fish:
And there the king is but as the beggar.

My brother Mourteen is worn out
With skelping his big brawling lout,
And I am running to Paradise;
A poor life, do what he can,
And though he keep a dog and a gun,
A serving-maid and a serving-man:
And there the king is but as the beggar.

Poor men have grown to be rich men,
And rich men grown to be poor again,
And I am running to Paradise;
And many a darling wit's grown dull
That tossed a bare heel when at school,
Now it has filled an old sock full:
And there the king is but as the beggar.

The wind is old and still at play
While I must hurry upon my way
For I am running to Paradise;
Yet never have I lit on a friend
To take my fancy like the wind
That nobody can buy or bind:
And there the king is but as the beggar.

W. B. YEATS

WILLIAM I
1066

William the First was the first of our kings,
Not counting Ethelreds, Egberts and things,
And he had himself crowned and anointed and blest
In Ten-Sixty-I-Needn't-Tell-You-The-Rest.

But being a Norman, King William the First
By the Saxons he conquered was hated and cursed,
And they planned and they plotted far into the night,
Which William could tell by the candles alight.

Then William decided these rebels to quell
By ringing the Curfew, a sort of a bell,
And if any Saxon was found out of bed
After eight o'clock sharp, it was Off With His Head!

So at BONG NUMBER ONE they all started to run
Like a warren of rabbits upset by a gun;
At BONG NUMBER TWO they were all in a stew,
Flinging cap after tunic and hose after shoe;

At BONG NUMBER THREE they were bare to the knee,
Undoing the doings as quick as could be;
At BONG NUMBER FOUR they were stripped to the core,
And pulling on nightshirts the wrong side before;
At BONG NUMBER FIVE they were looking alive,
And bizzing and buzzing like bees in a hive;
At BONG NUMBER SIX they gave themselves kicks,
Tripping over the rushes to snuff out the wicks;
At BONG NUMBER SEVEN, from Durham to Devon,
They slipped up a prayer to Our Father in Heaven;
And at BONG NUMBER EIGHT it was fatal to wait,
So with hearts beating all at a terrible rate,
In a deuce of a state, I need hardly relate,
They jumped BONG into bed like a bull at a gate.

ELEANOR & HERBERT FARJEON

THE LOOKING GLASS
A Country Dance

Queen Bess was Harry's daughter. Stand forward partners all!
In ruff and stomacher and gown
She danced King Philip down-a-down,
And left her shoe to show 'twas true —
  (The very tune I'm playing you)
In Norgem at Brickwall!

The Queen was in her chamber, and she was middling old.
Her petticoat was satin, and her stomacher was gold.
Backwards and forwards and sideways did she pass,
Making up her mind to face the cruel looking-glass.
The cruel looking-glass that will never show a lass
As comely or as kindly or as young as what she was!

Queen Bess was Harry's daughter. Now hand your partners all!

The Queen was in her chamber, a-combing of her hair.
There came Queen Mary's spirit and It stood behind her chair,
Singing 'Backwards and forwards and sideways may you pass,
But I will stand behind you till you face the looking-glass.
The cruel looking-glass that will never show a lass
As lovely or unlucky or as lonely as I was!'

Queen Bess was Harry's daughter. Now turn your partners all!

The Queen was in her chamber, a-weeping very sore,
There came Lord Leicester's spirit and It scratched upon the door,
Singing, 'Backwards and forwards and sideways may you pass,
But I will walk beside you till you face the looking-glass.
The cruel looking-glass that will never show a lass,
As hard and unforgiving or as wicked as you was!'

Queen Bess was Harry's daughter. Now kiss your partners all!

The Queen was in her chamber, her sins were on her head.
She looked the spirits up and down and statelily she said:—
'Backwards and forwards and sideways though I've been,
Yet I am Harry's daughter and I am England's Queen!'
And she faced the looking-glass (and whatever else there was)
And she saw her day was over and she saw her beauty pass
In the cruel looking-glass, that can always hurt a lass
More hard than any ghost there is or any man there was!

RUDYARD KIPLING

A pair of Queen Elizabeth's shoes are still at Brickwall House in England.

'WHEN I WAS FAIR AND YOUNG . . .'

When I was fair and young, and favour gracèd me,
Of many was I sought, their mistress for to be;
But I did scorn them all, and answered them therefore,
   'Go, go, go, seek some otherwhere,
   Importune me no more!'

How many weeping eyes I made to pine with woe,
How many sighing hearts, I have no skill to show;
Yet I the prouder grew, and answered them therefore,
   'Go, go, go, seek some otherwhere,
   Importune me no more!'

Then spake fair Venus' son, that proud victorious boy,
And said, 'Fine Dame, since that you be so coy,
I will so pluck your plumes that you shall say no more,
   Go, go, go, seek some otherwhere,
   Importune me no more!'

When he had spake these words, such change grew in my breast
That neither night nor day since that, I could take any rest.
Then lo, I did repent that I had said before,
   'Go, go, go, seek some otherwhere,
   Importune me no more!'

QUEEN ELIZABETH I OF ENGLAND

IMPROMPTU ON CHARLES II

God bless our good and gracious King,
    Whose promise none relies on;
Who never said a foolish thing,
    Nor ever did a wise one.

JOHN WILMOT, EARL OF ROCHESTER

*Charles II (restored to the English throne 1660, died
1685) did not take kindly to this rhyme, and
banished its author from court.*

ON PRINCE FREDERICK

Here lies Fred,
Who was alive and is dead:
Had it been his father,
I had much rather;
Had it been his brother,
Still better than another;
Had it been his sister,
No one would have missed her;
Had it been the whole generation,
So much the better for the nation:
But since 'tis only Fred,
Who was alive and is dead,
There's no more to be said.

ANONYMOUS

'I'M NOBODY! WHO ARE YOU?'

I'm Nobody! Who are you?
Are you – Nobody – too?
Then there's a pair of us!
Don't tell! they'd banish us – you know!

How dreary – to be – Somebody!
How public – like a Frog –
To tell your name – the livelong June –
To an admiring Bog!

EMILY DICKINSON

THE FROG PRINCE

I am a frog
I live under a spell
I live at the bottom
Of a green well

And here I must wait
Until a maiden places me
On her royal pillow
And kisses me
In her father's palace.

The story is familiar
Everybody knows it well
But do other enchanted people feel as nervous
As I do? The stories do not tell,

Ask if they will be happier
When the changes come
As already they are fairly happy
In a frog's doom?

I have been a frog now
For a hundred years
And in all this time
I have not shed many tears,

I am happy, I like the life,
Can swim for many a mile
(When I have hopped to the river)
And am for ever agile.

And the quietness,
Yes, I like to be quiet
I am habituated
To a quiet life,

But always when I think these thoughts
As I sit in my well
Another thought comes to me and says:
It is part of the spell

To be happy
To work up contentment
To make much of being a frog
To fear disenchantment

Says, It will be *heavenly*
To be set free,
Cries, *Heavenly* the girl who disenchants
And the royal times, *heavenly*,
And I think it will be.

Come then, royal girl and royal times,
Come quickly,
I can be happy until you come
But I cannot be heavenly,
Only disenchanted people
Can be heavenly.

STEVIE SMITH

TWO WEDDING SONGS

for HRH The Prince of Wales and Lady Diana Spencer
29 July 1981

I

Hang flags in the airs of July,
    Though the roses seem overblown
And the cuckoo stretches his wings to the south,
    And mark with a white stone
This date; set the bandsmen to play,
Touch off the exuberant fireworks –
    This is the wedding day:

For every wedding is royal,
    And royally affirms
Continuity and commitment;
    And though we are meat for worms
No more than dust and a shade,
    We dance between past and future,
With linked hands, unafraid.

II
London Birds: a Lollipop

'Why do those bell-tones crowd the air?'
Cooed the pigeons in Trafalgar Square.

'Because this is the bridal day,'
Said the white swan gliding on Thames broad way.

'Why fire in the sky, when it's meant to be dark?'
Cried the pelican in St James's Park.

'To show that the wedding knot is tied,'
Chirped the Cockney sparrows from Cheapside.

'Who is this couple so fêted and fond?'
Quacked the ducks on the Round Pond.

'Our Prince, and England's prettiest flower,'
Croaked an old black raven of the Tower.

JOHN HEATH-STUBBS

VAIN AND CARELESS

Lady, lovely lady,
 Careless and gay!
Once, when a beggar called,
 She gave her child away.

The beggar took the baby,
 Wrapped it in a shawl –
'Bring him back,' the lady said,
 'Next time you call.'

Hard by lived a vain man,
 So vain and so proud
He would walk on stilts
 To be seen by the crowd,

Up above the chimney pots,
 Tall as a mast –

And all the people ran about
 Shouting till he passed.

'A splendid match surely,'
 Neighbours saw it plain,
'Although she is so careless,
 Although he is so vain.'

But the lady played bobcherry,
 Did not see or care,
As the vain man went by her,
 Aloft in the air.

This gentle-born couple
 Lived and died apart –
Water will not mix with oil,
 Nor vain with careless heart.

ROBERT GRAVES

CUSHIE BUTTERFIELD

I's a broken-hearted keelman, and I's over head in love
With a young lass in Gateshead and I call her my dove.
Her name's Cushie Butterfield, and she sells yellow clay,
And her cousin is a muckman, and they call him Tom Grey.

    She's a big lass, and a bonny lass,
        And she likes her beer,
    And they call her Cushie Butterfield
        And I wish she was here.

Her eyes is like two holes in a blanket burnt through,
Her brows in a morning would spyen a young cow,
And when I hear her shouting, 'Will ye buy any clay?'
Like a candyman's trumpet, it steals my heart away.

Ye'll oft see her down at Sandgate when the fresh herring come in.
She's like a bag full of sawdust, tied round with a string.
She wears big galoshes too, and her stockings once was white,
And her petticoat's lilac, and her hat's never straight.

When I asked her to marry me she started to laugh;
'Now, none of your monkey tricks, for I don't like such chaff.'
Then she starts a-blubbering, and she roared like a bull,
And the chaps in the keel says I'm nowt but a fool.

She says the chap that gets her he must work every day,
And when he comes home at nights he must go and seek clay;
And when he's away seeking, she'll make balls and sing
'Oh well may the keel row that my laddie's in.'

    She's a big lass, and a bonny lass,
        And she likes her beer,
    And they call her Cushie Butterfield
        And I wish she was here.

GEORGE RIDLEY

THE WATER IS WIDE

The water is wide, I cannot get o'er,
And neither have I wings to fly.
Give me a boat that will carry two,
And both shall row, my love and I.

Down in the meadows the other day,
A-gathering flowers both fine and gay,
A-gathering flowers both red and blue
I little thought what love can do.

I leaned my back up against some oak,
Thinking that he was a trusty tree,
But first he bended and then he broke
And so did my false love to me.

I put my hand into the bush,
Thinking the fairest flower to find.
I pricked my finger to the bone,
But oh, I left the rose behind.

A ship there is and she sails the sea,
She's loaded deep as deep can be;
But not so deep as the love I'm in,
I know not if I sink or swim.

Love is handsome and love is kind,
And love's a jewel when she is new.
But when it is old, it groweth old
And fades away like the morning dew.

TRADITIONAL

A RED, RED ROSE

O my Luve's like a red, red rose,
    That's newly sprung in June.
O my Luve's like the melodie
    That's sweetly play'd in tune.

As fair art thou, my bonie lass,
    So deep in luve am I;
And I will love thee still, my Dear,
    Till a' the seas gang dry.

Till a' the seas gang dry, my Dear,
    And the rocks melt wi' the sun:
I will love thee still, my Dear,
    While the sands o' life shall run:

And fare thee weel, my only Luve!
    And fare thee weel, a while!
And I will come again, my Luve,
    Tho' it ware ten thousand mile!

ROBERT BURNS

gang: run

BALLAD OF AN OLD WOMAN

There was an old woman who never was wed;
Of twenty-one children was she brought to bed,
      Singing Glory to God.

She gave them all her poor means could afford
And brought them all up in the Fear of the Lord,
      Singing Glory to God.

As soon as they grew up, each sailed away,
One after the other to the great U.S.A.,
      Singing Glory to God.

Sometimes they thought of her, sometimes they wrote,
Sometimes they sent her a five dollar note:
      Singing Glory to God.

And when in the course of the long waiting years
The letters ceased coming, she dried her tears,
      Singing Glory to God.

And when the old shed-roof collapsed from decay
She went to the Almshouse and walked all the way,
      Singing Glory to God.

And there she mothered many motherless brats
Who slept on her shoulder and pulled at her plaits,
      Singing Glory to God.

Then one day she sickened and next day she died;
They brought out the hearse and put her inside
      Singing Glory to God.

Only weeds and nettles spring up from her clay
Who is one with the Night and the Light of the Day.
      Singing Glory to God.

FRANK COLLYMORE

A SONG ABOUT MYSELF

From a Letter to Fanny Keats

I

There was a naughty Boy,
   A naughty boy was he,
He would not stop at home,
   He could not quiet be –
      He took
      In his Knapsack
      A Book
      Full of vowels
      And a shirt
      With some towels –
      A slight cap
      For night cap –
      A hair brush,
      Comb ditto,
      New Stockings
      For old ones
      Would split O!
      This Knapsack
      Tight at's back
      He rivetted close
And followed his Nose
   To the North,
   To the North,
And followed his nose
   To the North.

II

There was a naughty boy
   And a naughty boy was he,
For nothing would he do
   But scribble poetry –
      He took
      An ink stand
      In his hand
      And a pen
      Big as ten
      In the other.
      And away
      In a Pother
      He ran
      To the mountains
      And fountains
      And ghostes
      And Postes
      And witches
      And ditches
      And wrote
      In his coat
      When the weather
      Was cool,
      Fear of gout,
      And without
      When the weather
      Was warm –
      Och the charm
      When we choose
To follow one's nose
   To the north,
   To the north,
To follow one's nose
   To the north!

III

There was a naughty boy
  And a naughty boy was he,
He kept little fishes
  In washing tubs three
    In spite
    Of the might
    Of the Maid
    Nor afraid
    Of his Granny-good –
    He often would
    Hurly burly
    Get up early
    And go
    By hook or crook
    To the brook
    And bring home
    Miller's thumb
    Tittlebat
    Not over fat,
    Minnows small
    As the stall
    Of a glove,
    Not above
    The size
    Of a nice
    Little Baby's
    Little fingers –
    O he made
    'Twas his trade
Of Fish a pretty Kettle
  A Kettle –
  A Kettle
Of Fish a pretty Kettle
  A Kettle!

IV

There was a naughty Boy,
  And a naughty Boy was he,
He ran away to Scotland
  The people for to see –
    Then he found
    That the ground
    Was as hard,
    That a yard
    Was as long,
    That a song
    Was as merry,
    That a cherry
    Was as red –
    That lead
    Was as weighty,
    That fourscore
    Was as eighty,
    That a door
    Was as wooden
    As in England –
So he stood in his shoes
  And he wondered
  He wondered,
He stood in his shoes
  And he wondered.

JOHN KEATS

HOW PLEASANT TO KNOW MR LEAR

'How pleasant to know Mr Lear!'
　　Who has written such volumes of stuff!
Some think him ill-tempered and queer,
　　But a few think him pleasant enough.

His mind is concrete and fastidious,
　　His nose is remarkably big;
His visage is more or less hideous,
　　His beard it resembles a wig.

He has ears, and two eyes, and ten fingers,
　　Leastways if you reckon two thumbs;
Long ago he was one of the singers,
　　But now he is one of the dumbs.

He sits in a beautiful parlour,
　　With hundreds of books on the wall
He drinks a great deal of Marsala,
　　But never gets tipsy at all.

He has many friends, laymen and clerical,
　　Old Foss is the name of his cat:
His body is perfectly spherical,
　　He weareth a runcible hat.

When he walks in a waterproof white,
　　The children run after him so!
Calling out, 'He's come out in his night-
　　gown, that crazy old Englishman, oh!'

He weeps by the side of the ocean,
　　He weeps on the top of the hill;
He purchases pancakes and lotion,
　　And chocolate shrimps from the mill.

He reads but he cannot speak Spanish,
　　He cannot abide ginger-beer:
Ere the days of his pilgrimage vanish,
　　How pleasant to know Mr Lear!

EDWARD LEAR

LINES FOR CUSCUSCARAWAY AND MIRZA MURAD ALI BEG

How unpleasant to meet Mr Eliot!
With his features of clerical cut,
And his brow so grim
And his mouth so prim
And his conversation, so nicely
Restricted to What Precisely
And If and Perhaps and But.
How unpleasant to meet Mr Eliot!
With a bobtail cur
In a coat of fur
And a porpentine cat
And a wopsical hat:
How unpleasant to meet Mr Eliot!
   (Whether his mouth be open or shut).

T. S. ELIOT

From SONG OF MYSELF

I celebrate myself, and sing myself,
And what I assume you shall assume,
For every atom belonging to me as good belongs to you.

I loafe and invite my soul,
I lean and loafe at my ease observing a spear of summer grass.

My tongue, every atom of my blood, form'd from this soil, this air,
Born here of parents born here from parents the same, and their parents the
    same,
I, now thirty-seven years old in perfect health begin,
Hoping to cease not till death.

Creeds and schools in abeyance,
Retiring back a while sufficed at what they are, but never forgotten,
I harbor for good or bad, I permit to speak at every hazard,
Nature without check with original energy.

WALT WHITMAN

ON HIS SEVENTY-FIFTH BIRTHDAY

I strove with none, for none was worth my strife,
   Nature I loved, and next to Nature, Art;
I warmed both hands before the fire of life,
   It sinks, and I am ready to depart.

WALTER SAVAGE LANDOR

'THE ART OF BIOGRAPHY'

The Art of Biography
Is different from Geography.
Geography is about Maps,
But Biography is about Chaps.

E. C. BENTLEY

*This is a 'clerihew': a verse
form invented by the author,
E. Clerihew Bentley*

POEM FOR A DEAD POET

He was a poet he was.
A proper poet.
He said things
that made you think
and said them nicely.
He saw things
that you or I
could never see
and saw them clearly.
He had a way
with language.
Images flocked around
him like birds,
St Francis, he was,
of the words. Words?
Why he could almost make 'em talk.

ROGER MCGOUGH

SAINT FRANCIS AND THE BIRDS

When Francis preached love to the birds
They listened, fluttered, throttled up
Into the blue like a flock of words

Released for fun from his holy lips.
Then wheeled back, whirred about his head,
Pirouetted on brothers' capes,

Danced on the wing, for sheer joy played
And sang, like images took flight.
Which was the best poem Francis made,

His argument true, his tone light.

SEAMUS HEANEY

LOVE WITHOUT HOPE

Love without hope, as when the young bird-catcher
Swept off his tall hat to the Squire's own daughter,
So let the imprisoned larks escape and fly
Singing about her head, as she rode by.

ROBERT GRAVES

WALKING SONG

The miles go sliding by
Under my steady feet,
That mark a leisurely
And still unbroken beat,
Through coppices that hear
Awhile, then lie as still
As though no traveller
Ever had climbed their hill.

My comrades are the small
Or dumb or singing birds,
Squirrels, field-things all
And placid drowsing herds.
Companions that I must
Greet for a while, then leave
Scattering the forward dust
From dawn to late of eve.

IVOR GURNEY

AFTERNOON TEA

Please you, excuse me, good five-o'clock people,
    I've lost my last hatful of words,
And my heart's in the wood up above the church steeple,
    I'd rather have tea with the birds.

Gay Kate's stolen kisses, poor Barnaby's scars,
    John's losses and Mary's gains,
Oh! what do they matter, my dears, to the stars
    Or the glow-worms in the lanes!

I'd rather lie under the tall elm-trees,
    With old rooks talking loud overhead,
To watch a red squirrel run over my knees,
    Very still on my brackeny bed.

And wonder what feathers the wrens will be taking
    For lining their nests next Spring;
Or why the tossed shadow of boughs in a great wind shaking
    Is such a lovely thing.

CHARLOTTE MEW

HOUSE FEAR

Always – I tell you this they learned –
Always at night when they returned
To the lonely house from far away,
To lamps unlighted and fire gone gray,
They learned to rattle the lock and key
To give whatever might chance to be,
Warning and time to be off in flight:
And preferring the out- to the indoor night,
They learned to leave the house door wide
Until they had lit the lamp inside.

ROBERT FROST

'ONE LEG . . .'

One leg in front of the other,
One leg in front of the other,
    As the little dog travelled
    From London to Dover.
And when he came to a stile –
    Jump! he went over.

TRADITIONAL

THIS IS JUST TO SAY

I have eaten
the plums
that were in
the icebox

and which
you were probably
saving
for breakfast

Forgive me
they were delicious
so sweet
and so cold

WILLIAM CARLOS WILLIAMS

WISHES OF AN ELDERLY MAN

I wish I loved the Human Race;
I wish I loved its silly face;
I wish I liked the way it walks;
I wish I liked the way it talks;
And when I'm introduced to one
I wish I thought *What Jolly Fun*!

WALTER RALEIGH

POEM AT THIRTY

it is midnight
no magical bewitching
hour for me
i know only that
i am here waiting
remembering that
once as a child
i walked two
miles in my sleep.
did i know
then where i
was going?
traveling. i'm
always traveling.
i want to tell
you about me
about nights on a
brown couch when
i wrapped my
bones in lint and
refused to move.
no one touches
me anymore.
father do not
send me out
among strangers.
you you black man
stretching scraping
the mold from your body.
here is my hand.
i am not afraid
of the night.

SONIA SANCHEZ

A RECOLLECTION

My father's friend came once to tea.
He laughed and talked. He spoke to me.
But in another week they said
That friendly pink-faced man was dead.

'How sad . .' they said, 'the best of men . .'
So I said too, 'How sad'; but then
Deep in my heart I thought with pride,
'I know a person who has died.'

FRANCES CORNFORD

A CONSUMER'S REPORT

The name of the product I tested is *Life*,
I have completed the form you sent me
and understand that my answers are confidential.
I had it as a gift,
I didn't feel much while using it,
in fact I think I'd have liked to be more excited.
It seemed gentle on the hands
but left an embarrassing deposit behind.
It was not economical
and I have used much more than I thought
(I suppose I have about half left
but it's difficult to tell) –
although the instructions are fairly large
there are so many of them
I don't know which to follow, especially
as they seem to contradict each other.
I'm not sure such a thing
should be put in the way of children –
It's difficult to think of a purpose
for it. One of my friends says
it's just to keep its maker in a job.
Also the price is much too high.
Things are piling up so fast,
after all, the world got by
for a thousand million years
without this, do we need it now?

(Incidentally, please ask your man
to stop calling me 'the respondent',
I don't like the sound of it.)
There seems to be a lot of different labels,
sizes and colours should be uniform,
the shape is awkward, it's waterproof
but not heat resistant, it doesn't keep
yet it's very difficult to get rid of:
whenever they make it cheaper they seem
to put less in – if you say you don't
want it, then it's delivered anyway.
I'd agree it's a popular product,
it's got into the language; people
even say they're on the side of it.
Personally I think it's overdone,
a small thing people are ready
to behave badly about. I think
we should take it for granted. If its
experts are called philosophers or market
researchers or historians, we shouldn't
care. We are the consumers and the last
law makers. So finally, I'd buy it.
But the question of a 'best buy'
I'd like to leave until I get
the competitive product you said you'd send.

PETER PORTER

'THE LAWS OF GOD, THE LAWS OF MAN'

The laws of God, the laws of man,
He may keep that will and can;
Not I: let God and man decree
Laws for themselves and not for me;
And if my ways are not as theirs
Let them mind their own affairs.
Their deeds I judge and much condemn,
Yet when did I make laws for them?
Please yourselves, say I, and they
Need only look the other way.
But no, they will not; they must still
Wrest their neighbour to their will,
And make me dance as they desire
With jail and gallows and hell-fire.
And how am I to face the odds
Of man's bedevilment and God's?
I, a stranger and afraid
In a world I never made.
They will be master, right or wrong;
Though both are foolish, both are strong.
And since, my soul, we cannot fly
To Saturn nor to Mercury,
Keep we must, if keep we can,
These foreign laws of God and man.

A. E. HOUSMAN

SONG: LIFT-BOY

Let me tell you the story of how I began:
I began as the knife-boy and ended as the boot-man,
With nothing in my pockets but a jack-knife and a button,
With nothing in my pockets but a jack-knife and a button,
With nothing in my pockets.

Let me tell you the story of how I went on:
I began as the lift-boy and ended as the lift-man,
With nothing in my pockets but a jack-knife and a button,
With nothing in my pockets but a jack-knife and a button,
With nothing in my pockets.

I found it very easy to whistle and play
With nothing in my head or my pockets all day,
With nothing in my pockets.
But along came Old Eagle, like Moses or David,
He stopped at the fourth floor and preached me Damnation:
'Not a soul shall be savèd, not one shall be savèd.
The whole First Creation shall forfeit salvation:
From knife-boy to lift-boy, from ragged to regal,
Not one shall be savèd, not you, not Old Eagle,
No soul on earth escapeth, even if all repent –'
So I cut the cords of the lift and down we went,
With nothing in our pockets.

ROBERT GRAVES

BIRDS AND BEASTS

THE HISTORY OF THE FLOOD

Bang Bang Bang
Said the nails in the Ark.

It's getting rather dark
Said the nails in the Ark.

For the rain is coming down
Said the nails in the Ark.

And you're all like to drown
Said the nails in the Ark.

Dark and black as sin
Said the nails in the Ark.

So won't you all come in
Said the nails in the Ark.

But only two by two
Said the nails in the Ark.

So they came in two by two,
The elephant, the kangaroo,
And the gnu,
And the little tiny shrew.

Then the birds
Flocked in like wingéd words:
Two racket-tailed motmots, two macaws,
Two nuthatches and two
Little bright robins.

And the reptiles: the gila monster, the slow-worm,
The green mamba, the cottonmouth and the alligator –
All squirmed in;
And after a very lengthy walk,
Two giant Galapagos tortoises.

And the insects in their hierarchies:
A queen ant, a king ant, a queen wasp, a king wasp,
A queen bee, a king bee,
And all the beetles, bugs, and mosquitoes,
Cascaded in like glittering, murmurous jewels.

But the fish had their wish;
For the rain came down.
People began to drown:
The wicked, the rich –
They gasped out bubbles of pure gold,
Which exhalations
Rose to the constellations.

So for forty days and forty nights
They were on the waste of waters
In those cramped quarters.
It was very dark, damp, and lonely.
There was nothing to see, but only
The rain which continued to drop.
It did not stop.

So Noah sent forth a Raven. The raven said 'Kark!

I will not go back to the Ark.'
The raven was footloose,
He fed on the bodies of the rich –
Rich with vitamins and goo.
They had become bloated,
And everywhere they floated.

The raven's heart was black,
He did not come back.
It was not a nice thing to do:
Which is why the raven is a token of wrath,
And creaks like a rusty gate
When he crosses your path; and Fate
Will grant you no luck that day:
The raven is fey:
You were meant to have a scare.
Fortunately in England
The raven is rather rare.

Then Noah sent forth a dove
She did not want to rove.
She longed for her love –
The other turtle dove –
(For her no other dove!)
She brought back a twig from an olive-tree.
There is no more beautiful tree
Anywhere on the earth,
Even when it comes to birth
From six weeks under the sea.

She did not want to rove.
She wanted to take her rest,
And to build herself a nest
All in the olive grove.
She wanted to make love.
She thought that was the best.

The dove was not a rover;
So they knew that the rain was over.
Noah and his wife got out

(They had become rather stout)
And Japhet, Ham, and Shem.
(The same could be said of them.)
They looked up at the sky.
The earth was becoming dry.

Then the animals came ashore –
There were more of them than before:
There were two dogs and a litter of puppies;
There were a tom-cat and two tib-cats
And two litters of kittens – cats
Do not obey regulations;
And, as you might expect,
A quantity of rabbits.

God put a rainbow in the sky.
They wondered what it was for.
There had never been a rainbow before.
The rainbow was a sign;
It looked like a neon sign –
Seven colours arched in the skies:
What should it publicize?
They looked up with wondering eyes.

It advertises Mercy
Said the nails in the Ark.

Mercy Mercy Mercy
Said the nails in the Ark.

Our God is merciful
Said the nails in the Ark.

Merciful and gracious
Bang Bang Bang Bang.

JOHN HEATH-STUBBS

THE LOVER WHOSE MISTRESS FEARED A MOUSE,
DECLARETH THAT HE WOULD BECOME A CAT,
IF HE MIGHT HAVE HIS DESIRE

If I might alter kind,
    what think you I would be?
Nor fish, nor fowl, nor flea, nor frog,
    nor squirrel on the tree.
The fish the hook, the fowl
    the limèd twig doth catch;
The flea the finger, and the frog
    the buzzard doth dispatch.
The squirrel thinking naught,
    that featly cracks the nut,
The greedy goshawk wanting prey
    in dread of death doth put.
But scorning all these kinds,
    I would become a cat,
To combat with the creeping mouse
    and scratch the screeking rat.
I would be present aye,
    and at my lady's call,
To guard her from the fearful mouse
    in parlour and in hall.
In kitchen for his life
    he should not show his head;
The pear in poke should lie untouched
    when she were gone to bed.
The mouse should stand in fear,
    so should the squeaking rat:
All this would I do if I were
    converted to a cat.

GEORGE TURBERVILLE

From JUBILATE AGNO

For I will consider my Cat Jeoffrey.

For he is the servant of the Living God, duly and daily serving him.

For at the First glance of the glory of God in the East he worships in his way.

For is this done by wreathing his body seven times round with elegant
quickness.

For then he leaps up to catch the musk, which is the blessing of God upon his
prayer.

For he rolls upon prank to work it in.

For having done duty and received blessing he begins to consider himself.

For this he performs in ten degrees.

For first he looks upon his fore-paws to see if they are clean.

For secondly he kicks up behind to clear away there.

For thirdly he works it upon stretch with the fore-paws extended.

For fourthly he sharpens his paws by wood.

For fifthly he washes himself.

For sixthly he rolls upon wash.

For Seventhly he fleas himself, that he may not be interrupted upon the beat.

For Eighthly he rubs himself against a post.

For Ninthly he looks up for his instructions.

For Tenthly he goes in quest of food.

For having consider'd God and himself he will consider his neighbour.

For if he meets another cat he will kiss her in kindness.

For when he takes his prey he plays with it to give it a chance.

For one mouse in seven escapes by his dallying.

For when his day's work is done his business more properly begins.

For he keeps the Lord's watch in the night against the adversary.

For he counteracts the powers of darkness by his electrical skin & glaring eyes.

For he counteracts the Devil, who is death, by brisking about the life.

For in his morning orisons he loves the sun and the sun loves him.

For he is of the tribe of Tiger.

For the Cherub Cat is a term of the Angel Tiger.

For he has the subtlety and hissing of a serpent, which in goodness he
suppresses.

For he will not do destruction, if he is well fed, neither will he spit without
provocation.

For he purrs in thankfulness, when God tells him he's a good Cat.

For he is an instrument for the children to learn benevolence upon.

For every house is incomplete without him and a blessing is lacking in the
spirit.

For the Lord commanded Moses concerning the cats at the departure of the
Children of Israel from Egypt.

For every family had one cat at least in the bag.

For the English Cats are the best in Europe.

For he is the cleanest in the use of his fore-paws of any quadrupede.

For the dexterity of his defence is an instance of the love of God to him
exceedingly.

For he is the quickest to his mark of any creature.

For he is tenacious of his point.

For he is a mixture of gravity and waggery.

For he knows that God is his Saviour.

For there is nothing sweeter than his peace when at rest.

For there is nothing brisker than his life in motion.

For he is of the Lord's poor and so indeed is he called by benevolence
perpetually – Poor Jeoffrey! poor Jeoffrey! the rat has bit thy throat.

For I bless the name of the Lord Jesus that Jeoffrey is better.

For the divine spirit comes about his body to sustain it in complete cat.

For his tongue is exceedingly pure so that it has in purity what it wants in
music.

For he is docile and can learn certain things.

For he can set up with gravity which is patience upon approbation.

For he can fetch and carry, which is patience in employment.

For he can jump over a stick which is patience upon proof positive.

For he can spraggle upon waggle at the word of command.

For he can jump from an eminence into his master's bosom.

For he can catch the cork and toss it again.

For he is hated by the hypocrite and miser.

For the former is affraid of detection.

For the latter refuses the charge.

For he camels his back to bear the first notion of business.

For he is good to think on, if a man would express himself neatly.

For he made a great figure in Egypt for his signal services.

For he killed the Ichneumon-rat very pernicious by land.

For his ears are so acute that they sting again.

For from this proceeds the passing quickness of his attention.

For by stroking of him I have found out electricity.

For I perceived God's light upon him both wax and fire.

For the Electrical fire is the spiritual substance, which God sends from heaven
to sustain the bodies both of man and beast.

For God has blessed him in the variety of his movements.

For, tho he cannot fly, he is an excellent clamberer.

For his motions upon the face of the earth are more than any other
quadrupede.

For he can tread to all the measures upon the music.

For he can swim for life.

For he can creep.

CHRISTOPHER SMART

*Christopher Smart wrote this poem while confined in a
mental asylum. Most of his poems are works of
prayer or praise.*

THE RUM TUM TUGGER

The Rum Tum Tugger is a Curious Cat:
If you offer him pheasant he would rather have grouse.
If you put him in a house he would much prefer a flat,
If you put him in a flat then he'd rather have a house.
If you set him on a mouse then he only wants a rat,
If you set him on a rat then he'd rather chase a mouse.
Yes the Rum Tum Tugger is a Curious Cat —

And there isn't any call for me to shout it:
   For he will do
   As he do do
      And there's no doing anything about it!

The Rum Tum Tugger is a terrible bore:
When you let him in, then he wants to be out;
He's always on the wrong side of every door,
And as soon as he's at home, then he'd like to get about.
He likes to lie in the bureau drawer,
But he makes such a fuss if he can't get out.
Yes the Rum Tum Tugger is a Curious Cat —
   And it isn't any use for you to doubt it:
    For he will do
    As he do do
      And there's no doing anything about it!

The Rum Tum Tugger is a curious beast:
His disobliging ways are a matter of habit.
If you offer him fish then he always wants a feast;
When there isn't any fish then he won't eat rabbit.
If you offer him cream then he sniffs and sneers,
For he only likes what he finds for himself;
So you'll catch him in it right up to the ears,
If you put it away on the larder shelf.
The Rum Tum Tugger is artful and knowing,
The Rum Tum Tugger doesn't care for a cuddle;
But he'll leap on your lap in the middle of your sewing,
For there's nothing he enjoys like a horrible muddle.
Yes the Rum Tum Tugger is a Curious Cat —
   And there isn't any need for me to spout it:
    For he will do
    As he do do
      And there's no doing anything about it!

            T. S. ELIOT

ON THE DEATH OF A MAD DOG

Good people all, of every sort,
   Give ear unto my song;
And if you find it wondrous short,
   It cannot hold you long.

In Islington there was a man,
   Of whom the world might say,
That still a godly race he ran,
   Whene'er he went to pray.

A kind and gentle heart he had,
   To comfort friends and foes;
The naked every day he clad,
   When he put on his clothes.

And in that town a dog was found,
   As many dogs there be,
Both mongrel, puppy, whelp, and hound,
   And curs of low degree.

This dog and man at first were friends;
   But when a pique began,
The dog, to gain his private ends,
   Went mad, and bit the man.

Around from all the neighbouring streets
   The wondering neighbours ran,
And swore the dog had lost his wits,
   To bite so good a man.

The wound it seemed both sore and sad
   To every Christian eye;
And while they swore the dog was mad,
   They swore the man would die.

But soon a wonder came to light,
   That showed the rogues they lied;
The man recovered of the bite,
   The dog it was that died.

      OLIVER GOLDSMITH

THE CAT

His kind velvet bonnet
Warmly lies upon
My weary lap, and on it
My tears run.

The black and furry fire
Sinks low, and like the dire
Sound of charring coal, the black
Cat's whirring back.

On the bare bough
A few blue threadbare leaves,
A few blue plaided leaves grow
Like mornings and like eves.

Scotch bonnet, bonny,
Lying on my gown,
The fire was once, hey nonny,
A battlemented town;

And every morn I build
Those steep castles there,
And every night they're ruined
Like the boughs bare.

And nothing doth remain,
Kind bonny, but my pain,
And night and morn, like boughs they're bare,
With nobody to care.

      EDITH SITWELL

HARES AT PLAY

The birds are gone to bed, the cows are still,
And sheep lie panting on each old mole-hill;
And underneath the willow's grey-green bough,
Like toil a-resting, lies the fallow plough.
The timid hares throw daylight fears away
On the lane's road to dust and dance and play,
Then dabble in the grain by naught deterred
To lick the dew-fall from the barley's beard;
Then out they sturt again and round the hill
Like happy thoughts dance, squat, and loiter still,
Till milking maidens in the early morn
Jingle their yokes and sturt them in the corn;
Through well-known beaten paths each nimbling hare
Sturts quick as fear, and seeks its hidden lair.

JOHN CLARE

sturt: start

FISH

A fish dripping
sparkling drops
of crystal water,
pulled from the lake;
long has it dwelt
in the cool water,
in the cold water
of the lake.

Long has it wandered
to and fro
over the bottom
of the lake
among mysterious
recesses
there in the semi-
light of the water;

now to appear
surprised, aghast,
out of its element
into the day; –
out of the cold
and shining lake
the fish dripping
sparkling water.

W. W. E. ROSS

THE OYSTER

The herring loves the merry moonlight,
  The mackerel loves the wind;
But the oyster loves the dredging-sang,
  For they come of a gentle kind.

TRADITIONAL

A dredging-song was a meaningless ditty sung by Scottish
fishermen to encourage the catch; oysters were supposed to
like being sung to.

THE FISH

I caught a tremendous fish
and held him beside the boat
half out of water, with my hook
fast in a corner of his mouth.
He didn't fight.
He hadn't fought at all.
He hung a grunting weight,
battered and venerable
and homely. Here and there
his brown skin hung in strips
like ancient wall-paper,
and its pattern of darker brown
was like wall-paper:
shapes like full-blown roses
stained and lost through age.
He was speckled with barnacles,
fine rosettes of lime,
and infested
with tiny white sea-lice,
and underneath two or three
rags of green weed hung down.
While his gills were breathing in
the terrible oxygen
– the frightening gills
fresh and crisp with blood,
that can cut so badly –
I thought of the coarse white flesh
packed in like feathers,
the big bones and the little bones,
the dramatic reds and blacks
of his shiny entrails,
and the pink swim-bladder
like a big peony.
I looked into his eyes
which were far larger than mine
but shallower, and yellowed,
the irises backed and packed
with tarnished tinfoil
seen through the lenses
of old scratched isinglass.
They shifted a little, but not
to return my stare.
– It was more like the tipping
of an object toward the light.
I admired his sullen face,
the mechanism of his jaw,
and then I saw
that from his lower lip
– if you could call it a lip –
grim, wet, and weapon-like,
hung five old pieces of fish-line
or four and a wire leader
with the swivel still attached,
with all their five big hooks
grown firmly in his mouth.
A green line, frayed at the end
where he broke it, two heavier lines,
and a fine black thread
still crimped from the strain and snap
when it broke and he got away.
Like medals with their ribbons
frayed and wavering,
a five-haired beard of wisdom
trailing from his aching jaw.
I stared and stared
and victory filled up
the little rented boat,
from the pool of bilge
where oil had spread a rainbow
around the rusted engine
to the bailer rusted orange,
the sun-cracked thwarts,
the oarlocks on their strings,
the gunnels – until everything
was rainbow, rainbow, rainbow!
And I let the fish go.

ELIZABETH BISHOP

THREE SONNETS

To a Fish

You strange, astonished-looking, angle-faced,
Dreary-mouthed, gaping wretches of the sea,
Gulping salt water everlastingly,
Cold-blooded, though with red your blood be graced,
And mute, though dwellers in the roaring waste;
And you, all shapes beside, that fishy be –
Some round, some flat, some long, all devilry,
Legless, unloving, infamously chaste:

O scaly, slippery, wet, swift, staring wights,
What is't ye do? What life lead? eh, dull goggles?
How do ye vary your vile days and nights?
How pass your Sundays? Are ye still but joggles
In ceaseless wash? Still nought but gapes, and bites,
And drinks, and stares, diversified with boggles?

A Fish replies

Amazing monster! that, for aught I know,
With the first sight of thee didst make our race
For ever stare! O flat and shocking face,
Grimly divided from the breast below!
Thou that on dry land horribly dost go
With a split body and most ridiculous pace,
Prong after prong, disgracer of all grace,
Long-useless-finned, haired, upright, unwet, slow!

O breather of unbreathable, sword-sharp air,
How canst exist? How 'bear thyself, thou dry
And dreary sloth? What particle canst share
Of the only blessed life, the watery?
I sometimes see of ye an actual *pair*
Go by, linked fin by fin, most odiously.

The Fish turns into a Man, and then into a Spirit,
and again speaks

Indulge thy smiling scorn, if smiling still,
O man! and loathe, but with a sort of love;
For difference must its use by difference prove,
And, in sweet clang, the spheres with music fill.
One of the spirits am I, that at his will
Live in whate'er has life – fish, eagle, dove –
No hate, no pride, beneath naught, nor above,
A visitor of the rounds of God's sweet skill.

Man's life is warm, glad, sad, 'twixt loves and graves,
Boundless in hope, honoured with pangs austere,
Heaven-gazing; and his angel-wings he craves:
The fish is swift, small-needing, vague yet clear,
A cold, sweet, silver life, wrapped in round waves,
Quickened with touches of transporting fear.

LEIGH HUNT

TO A BUTTERFLY

I've watched you now a full half-hour,
Self-poised upon that yellow flower;
And, little Butterfly! indeed
I know not if you sleep or feed.
How motionless! – not frozen seas
More motionless! And then
What joy awaits you, when the breeze
Hath found you out among the trees,
And calls you forth again!

This plot of orchard-ground is ours;
My trees they are, my Sister's flowers.
Here rest your wings when they are weary;
Here lodge as in a sanctuary!
Come often to us, fear no wrong;
Sit near us on the bough!
We'll talk of sunshine and of song,
And summer days, when we were young;
Sweet childish days, that were as long
As twenty days are now.

WILLIAM WORDSWORTH

ANSWER TO A CHILD'S QUESTION

Do you ask what the birds say? The Sparrow, the Dove,
The Linnet and Thrush say, 'I love and I love!'
In the winter they're silent – the wind is so strong;
What it says, I don't know, but it sings a loud song.
But green leaves, and blossoms, and sunny warm weather,
And singing, and loving – all come back together.
But the Lark is so brimful of gladness and love,
The green fields below him, the blue sky above,
That he sings, and he sings; and for ever sings he –
'I love my Love, and my Love loves me!'

S. T. COLERIDGE

ALLIE

Allie, call the birds in,
    The birds from the sky!
Allie calls, Allie sings,
    Down they all fly:
First there came
Two white doves,
    Then a sparrow from his nest,
Then a clucking bantam hen,
    Then a robin red-breast.

Allie, call the beasts in,
    The beasts, everyone!
Allie calls, Allie sings,
    In they all run:
First there came
Two black lambs,
    Then a grunting Berkshire sow,
Then a dog without a tail,
    Then a red and white cow.

Allie, call the fish up,
    The fish from the stream!
Allie calls, Allie sings,
    Up they all swim:
First there came
Two goldfish,
    A minnow and a miller's thumb,
Then a school of little trout,
    Then the twisting eels come.

Allie, call the children,
    Call them from the green!
Allie calls, Allie sings,
    Soon they run in:
First there came
Tom and Madge,
    Kate and I who'll not forget
How we played by the water's edge
    Till the April sun set.

ROBERT GRAVES

LITTLE TROTTY WAGTAIL

Little trotty wagtail he went in the rain
And tittering tottering sideways he near got straight again
He stooped to get a worm and look'd up to catch a fly
And then he flew away e're his feathers they were dry

Little trotty wagtail he waddled in the mud
And left his little foot marks trample where he would
He waddled in the water pudge and waggle went his tail
And chirrup up his wings to dry upon the garden rail

Little trotty wagtail you nimble all about
And in the dimpling water pudge you waddle in and out
Your home is nigh at hand and in the warm pigsty
So little Master Wagtail I'll bid you a 'Good bye'

JOHN CLARE

ROBIN REDBREAST'S TESTAMENT

'Guid-day now, bonnie Robin,
    How lang have you been here?'
'I've been bird about this bush
    This mair than twenty year!

        Teetle ell ell, teetle ell ell,
        Teetle ell ell, teetle ell ell;
        Tee tee tee tee tee tee tee,
            Tee tee tee tee, teetle eldie.

'But now I am the sickest bird
    That ever sat on brier;
And I wad make my testament,
    Guidman, if ye wad hear.

'Gar tak this bonnie neb o' mine,
    That picks upon the corn,
And gie't to the Duke o' Hamilton
    To be a hunting-horn.

'Gar tak these bonnie feathers o' mine,
    The feathers o' my neb,
And gie to the Lady o' Hamilton
    To fill a feather-bed.

'Gar tak this guid right leg o' mine,
    And mend the brig o' Tay;
It will be a post and pillar guid –
    It will neither bow nor gae.

'And tak this other leg o' mine,
    And mend the brig o' Weir;
It will be a post and pillar guid –
    It'll neither bow nor steer.

'Gar tak these bonnie feathers o' mine,
    The feathers o' my tail,
And gie to the lads o' Hamilton
    To be a barn flail.

'And tak these bonnie feathers o' mine,
    The feathers o' my breast,
And gie to ony bonnie lad
    That'll bring to me a priest.'

Now in there came my Lady Wren,
    With mony a sigh and groan;
'O what care I for a' the lads,
    If my wee lad be gone?'

Then Robin turned him round about,
    E'en like a little king;
'Go, pack ye out at my chamber-door,
    Ye little cutty quean.'

Robin made his testament
    Upon a coll of hay,
And by came a greedy gled,
    And snapt him a' away.

        Teetle ell ell, teetle ell ell,
        Teetle ell ell, teetle ell ell;
        Tee tee tee tee tee tee tee,
            Tee tee tee tee, teetle eldie.

TRADITIONAL

*This is a Scottish robin. Neb: beak. Brig: bridge.
Cutty quean: naughty little girl, often used as a name
for the wren. Coll: cock or rick of hay.
Gled: a kite or similar bird of prey.*

'REPEAT THAT, REPEAT'

Repeat that, repeat,
Cuckoo, bird, and open ear wells, heart-springs,
   delightfully sweet,
With a ballad, with a ballad, a rebound
Off trundled timber and scoops of the hillside ground,
   hollow hollow hollow ground:
The whole landscape flushes on a sudden at a sound.

GERARD MANLEY HOPKINS

*This is not a finished poem but a fragment
found among the poet's papers.*

ON THE CUCKOO

The idle cuckoo, having made a feast
On sparrows' eggs, lays down her own i'th'nest;
The silly bird she owns it, hatches, feeds it,
Protects it from the weather, clocks and breeds it;
It neither wants repose nor yet repast,
And joys to see her chicken thrive so fast:
But when this gaping monster has found strength
To shift without a helper, she at length,
Nor caring for that tender care that bred her,
Forgets her parent, kills the bird that fed her:
The sin we foster in our bosom, thus,
Ere we have left to feed it, feeds on us.

FRANCIS QUARLES

clocks: hatches

THE CUCKOO

The cuckoo is a merry bird,
   She sings as she flies;
She brings us good tidings,
   And tells us no lies.

She sucks little birds' eggs
   To make her voice clear,
That she may sing Cuckoo!
   Three months in the year.

TRADITIONAL

WILTSHIRE DOWNS

The cuckoo's double note
Loosened like bubbles from a drowning throat
Floats through the air
In mockery of pipit, lark and stare.

The stable-boys thud by
Their horses slinging divots at the sky
And with bright hooves
Printing the sodden turf with lucky grooves.

As still as a windhover
A shepherd in his flapping coat leans over
His tall sheep-crook
And shearlings, tegs and yoes cons like a book.

And one tree-crowned long barrow
Stretched like a sow that has brought forth her farrow
Hides a king's bones
Lying like broken sticks among the stones.

ANDREW YOUNG

divots: pieces of turf; shearlings, tegs and yoes: sheep
barrow: ancient burial mound

THE EAGLE

He clasps the crag with crooked hands;
Close to the sun in lonely lands,
Ring'd with the azure world, he stands.

The wrinkled sea beneath him crawls;
He watches from his mountain walls,
And like a thunderbolt he falls.

ALFRED TENNYSON

THE FOWLER

A wild bird filled the morning air
With dewy-hearted song:
I took it in a golden snare
With meshes close and strong.

But where is now the song I heard?
For all my cunning art,
I who would house a singing-bird
Have caged a broken heart.

WILFRID GIBSON

MICHAEL'S SONG

Because I set no snare
But leave them flying free,
All the birds of the air
Belong to me.

From the bluetit on the sloe
To the eagle on the height
Uncaged they come and go
For my delight.

And so the sunward way
I soar on the eagle's wings,
And in my heart all day
The bluetit sings.

WILFRID GIBSON

'A NARROW FELLOW
IN THE GRASS'

A narrow Fellow in the Grass
Occasionally rides –
You may have met Him – did you not
His notice sudden is –

The Grass divides as with a Comb –
A spotted shaft is seen –
And then it closes at your feet
And opens further on –

He likes a Boggy Acre
A Floor too cool for Corn –
Yet when a Boy, and Barefoot –
I more than once at Noon
Have passed, I thought, a Whip lash
Unbraiding in the Sun
When stooping to secure it
It wrinkled, and was gone –

Several of Nature's People
I know, and they know me –
I feel for them a transport
Of cordiality –

But never met this Fellow
Attended, or alone
Without a tighter breathing
And Zero at the Bone –

EMILY DICKINSON

SNAKE

A snake came to my water-trough
On a hot, hot day, and I in pyjamas for the heat,
To drink there.

In the deep, strange-scented shade of the great dark carob-tree
I came down the steps with my pitcher
And must wait, must stand and wait, for there he was at the trough before me

He reached down from a fissure in the earth-wall in the gloom
And trailed his yellow-brown slackness soft-bellied down, over the edge of the
        stone trough
And rested his throat upon the stone bottom,
And where the water had dripped from the tap, in a small clearness,
He sipped with his straight mouth,
Softly drank through his straight gums, into his slack long body,
Silently.

Someone was before me at my water-trough,
And I, like a second-comer, waiting.

He lifted his head from his drinking, as cattle do,
And looked at me vaguely, as drinking cattle do,
And flickered his two-forked tongue from his lips, and mused a moment,
And stooped and drank a little more,
Being earth-brown, earth-golden from the burning bowels of the earth
On the day of Sicilian July, with Etna smoking.

The voice of my education said to me
He must be killed,
For in Sicily the black, black snakes are innocent, the gold are venomous.

And voices in me said, If you were a man
You would take a stick and break him now, and finish him off.

But must I confess how I liked him,
How glad I was he had come like a guest in quiet, to drink at my water-trough
And depart peaceful, pacified and thankless,
Into the burning bowels of this earth?

Was it cowardice, that I dared not kill him?
Was it perversity, that I longed to talk to him?
Was it humility, to feel so honoured?
I felt so honoured.

And yet those voices:
If you were not afraid, you would kill him!

And truly I was afraid, I was most afraid,
But even so, honoured still more
That he should seek my hospitality
From out the dark door of the secret earth.

He drank enough
And lifted his head, dreamily, as one who has drunken,
And flickered his tongue like a forked night on the air, so black,
Seeming to lick his lips,
And looked around like a god, unseeing, into the air,
And slowly turned his head,
And slowly, very slowly, as if thrice adream,
Proceeded to draw his slow length curving round
And climb again the broken bank of my wall-face.

And as he put his head into that dreadful hole,
And as he slowly drew up, snake-easing his shoulders, and entered farther,
A sort of horror, a sort of protest against his withdrawing into that horrid black
     hole,
Deliberately going into the blackness, and slowly drawing himself after,
Overcame me now his back was turned.

I looked round, I put down my pitcher,
I picked up a clumsy log
And threw it at the water-trough with a clatter.

I think it did not hit him,
But suddenly that part of him that was left behind convulsed in undignified
     haste,
Writhed like lightning, and was gone
Into the black hole, the earth-lipped fissure in the wall-front,
At which, in the intense still noon, I stared with fascination.

And immediately I regretted it.
I thought how paltry, how vulgar, what a mean act!
I despised myself and the voices of my accursed human education.

And I thought of the albatross,
And I wished he would come back, my snake.

For he seemed to me again like a king,
Like a king in exile, uncrowned in the underworld,
Now due to be crowned again.

And so, I missed my chance with one of the lords
Of life.
And I have something to expiate:
A pettiness.

D. H. LAWRENCE

LIZARD

A lizard ran out on a rock and looked up, listening
no doubt to the sounding of the spheres.
And what a dandy fellow! the right toss of a chin for you
and swirl of a tail!

If men were as much men as lizards are lizards
they'd be worth looking at.

D. H. LAWRENCE

THE BULL MOOSE

Down from the purple mist of trees on the mountain,
lurching through forests of white spruce and cedar,
stumbling through tamarack swamps,
came the bull moose
to be stopped at last by a pole-fenced pasture.

Too tired to turn or, perhaps, aware
there was no place left to go, he stood with the cattle.
They, scenting the musk of death, seeing his great head
like the ritual mask of a blood god, moved to the other end
of the field, and waited.

The neighbours heard of it, and by afternoon
cars lined the road. The children teased him
with alder switches and he gazed at them
like an old, tolerant collie. The women asked
if he could have escaped from a Fair.

The oldest man in the parish remembered seeing
a gelded moose yoked with an ox for plowing.
The young men snickered and tried to pour beer
down his throat, while their girl friends took their pictures.

And the bull moose let them stroke his tick-ravaged flanks,
let them pry open his jaws with bottles, let a giggling girl
plant a little purple cap
of thistles on his head.

When the wardens came, everyone agreed it was a shame
to shoot anything so shaggy and cuddlesome.
He looked like the kind of pet
women put to bed with their sons.

So they held their fire. But just as the sun dropped in the river
the bull moose gathered his strength
like a scaffolded king, straightened and lifted his horns
so that even the wardens backed away as they raised their rifles.
When he roared, people ran to their cars. All the young men
leaned on their automobile horns as he toppled.

ALDEN NOWLAN

THE THOUGHT-FOX

I imagine this midnight moment's forest:
Something else is alive
Beside the clock's loneliness
And this blank page where my fingers move.

Through the window I see no star:
Something more near
Though deeper within darkness
Is entering the loneliness:

Cold, delicately as the dark snow
A fox's nose touches twig, leaf;
Two eyes serve a movement, that now
And again now, and now, and now

Sets neat prints into the snow
Between trees, and warily a lame
Shadow lags by stump and in hollow
Of a body that is bold to come

Across clearings, an eye,
A widening deepening greenness,
Brilliantly, concentratedly,
Coming about its own business

Till, with a sudden sharp hot stink of fox
It enters the dark hole of the head.
The window is starless still; the clock ticks,
The page is printed.

TED HUGHES

*Ted Hughes writes, 'every time I read the poem the fox
comes up again out of the darkness and steps into my head.
And I suppose that long after I am gone, as long as a copy
of the poem exists, every time anyone reads it the fox will
get up somewhere out in the darkness and come walking
towards them.'*

THE TYGER

Tyger! Tyger! burning bright
In the forests of the night,
What immortal hand or eye
Could frame thy fearful symmetry?

In what distant deeps or skies
Burnt the fire of thine eyes?
On what wings dare he aspire?
What the hand dare sieze the fire?

And what shoulder, and what art,
Could twist the sinews of thy heart?
And when thy heart began to beat,
What dread hand? and what dread feet?

What the hammer? what the chain?
In what furnace was thy brain?
What the anvil? what dread grasp
Dare its deadly terrors clasp?

When the stars threw down their spears,
And water'd heaven with their tears,
Did he smile his work to see?
Did he who made the Lamb make thee?

Tyger! Tyger! burning bright
In the forests of the night,
What immortal hand or eye
Dare frame thy fearful symmetry?

WILLIAM BLAKE

A NOISELESS PATIENT SPIDER

A noiseless patient spider,
I mark'd where on a little promontory it stood isolated,
Mark'd how to explore the vacant vast surrounding,
It launch'd forth filament, filament, filament, out of itself,
Ever unreeling them, ever tirelessly speeding them.

And you O my soul where you stand,
Surrounded, detached, in measureless oceans of space,
Ceaselessly musing, venturing, throwing, seeking the spheres to connect them,
Till the bridge you will need be form'd, till the ductile anchor hold,
Till the gossamer thread you fling catch somewhere, O my soul.

WALT WHITMAN

'YESTERDAY HE WAS NOWHERE TO BE FOUND'

Yesterday he was nowhere to be found
In the skies or under the skies.
Suddenly he's here – a warm heap
Of ashes and embers, fondled by small draughts.

A star dived from outer space – flared
And burned out in the straw.
Now something is stirring in the smoulder.
We call it a foal.

Still stunned
He has no idea where he is.
His eyes, dew-dusky, explore gloom walls and a glare doorspace.
Is this the world?
It puzzles him. It is a great numbness.

He pulls himself together, getting used to the weight of things
And to that tall horse nudging him, and to this straw.

He rests
From the first blank shock of light, the empty daze
Of the questions –
What has happened? What am I?

His ears keep on asking, gingerly.

But his legs are impatient,
Recovering from so long being nothing
They are restless with ideas, they start to try a few out,
Angling this way and that,
Feeling for leverage, learning fast –

And suddenly he's up

And stretching – a giant hand
Strokes him from nose to heel
Perfecting his outline, as he tightens
The knot of himself.
                                Now he comes teetering
Over the weird earth. His nose
Downy and magnetic, draws him, incredulous,
Towards his mother. And the world is warm
And careful and gentle. Touch by touch
Everything fits him together.

Soon he'll be almost a horse.
He wants only to be Horse,
Pretending each day more and more Horse
Till he's perfect Horse. Then unearthly Horse
Will surge through him, weightless, a spinning of flame
Under sudden gusts,

It will coil his eyeball and his heel
In a single terror – like the awe
Between lightning and thunderclap.

And curve his neck, like a sea-monster emerging
Among foam,

And fling the new moons through his stormy banner,
And the full moons and the dark moons.

TED HUGHES

POOR OLD HORSE

Once I was a young horse all in my youthful prime,
My mane hung o'er my shoulders and my coat he did so shine;
But now I'm getting old, my features do decay,
My master he looks down on me and his words I heard him say:

Poor old horse, poor old horse,
Poor old horse, let him die.

My master used to ride me at every chase all round,
My legs they were so nimble I could trip over the ground,
But now I'm getting old and scarcely able to crawl,
My master he looks down on me, saying I am no use at all.

Once all in the stable I used good corn and hay
That grows in yonder fields and likewise meadows so gay.
But now I'm getting old I scarcely get hay at all,
For I'm obliged to nibble the short grass that grows against the wall.

Once all in the stable I was kept so fine and warm
To keep my tender limbs from all aching pain and harm,
But now I'm getting old to the fields I'm obliged to go,
Let it hail, rain or sunshine, or the winds blow high or low.

My hide unto the huntsman so freely will I give,
My body to the hounds, for I'd rather die than live,
Then lay my legs so low that have run so many a mile,
Over the hedges, over ditches, over turnpike gates and stiles.

Poor old horse, poor old horse,
Poor old horse, let him die.

TRADITIONAL

SHEEP

When I was once in Baltimore,
    A man came up to me and cried,
'Come, I have eighteen hundred sheep,
    And we will sail on Tuesday's tide.

'If you will sail with me, young man,
    I'll pay you fifty shillings down;
These eighteen hundred sheep I take
    From Baltimore to Glasgow town.'

He paid me fifty shillings down,
    I sailed with eighteen hundred sheep;

We soon had cleared the harbour's mouth,
    We soon were in the salt sea deep.

The first night we were out at sea
    Those sheep were quiet in their mind;
The second night they cried with fear –
    They smelt no pastures in the wind.

They sniffed, poor things, for their green fields,
    They cried so loud I could not sleep:
For fifty thousand shillings down
    I would not sail again with sheep.

W. H. DAVIES

MILKING BEFORE DAWN

In the drifting rain the cows in the yard are as black
And wet and shiny as rocks in an ebbing tide;
But they smell of the soil, as leaves lying under trees
Smell of the soil, damp and steaming, warm.
The shed is an island of light and warmth, the night
Was water-cold and starless out in the paddock.

Crouched on the stool, hearing only the beat
The monotonous beat and hiss of the smooth machines,
The choking gasp of the cups and rattle of hooves,
How easy to fall asleep again, to think
Of the man in the city asleep; he does not feel
The night encircle him, the grasp of mud.

But now the hills in the east return, are soft
And grey with mist, the night recedes, and the rain.
The earth as it turns towards the sun is young
Again, renewed, its history wiped away
Like the tears of a child. Can the earth be young again
And not the heart? Let the man in the city sleep.

RUTH DALLAS

COWS

Half the time they munched the grass, and all the time they lay
Down in the water-meadows, the lazy month of May,
    A-chewing,
    A-mooing,
To pass the hours away.

'Nice weather,' said the brown cow.
  'Ah,' said the white.
'Grass is very tasty.'
  'Grass is all right.'

Half the time they munched the grass, and all the time they lay
Down in the water-meadows, the lazy month of May,
    A-chewing,
    A-mooing,
To pass the hours away.

'Rain coming,' said the brown cow.
  'Ah,' said the white.
'Flies is very tiresome.'
  'Flies bite.'

Half the time they munched the grass, and all the time they lay
Down in the water-meadows, the lazy month of May,
    A-chewing,
    A-mooing,
To pass the hours away.

'Time to go,' said the brown cow.
  'Ah,' said the white.
'Nice chat.' 'Very pleasant.'
  'Night.' 'Night.'

Half the time they munched the grass, and all the time they lay
Down in the water-meadows, the lazy month of May,
    A-chewing,
    A-mooing,
To pass the hours away.

JAMES REEVES

THE OXEN

Christmas Eve, and twelve of the clock.
    'Now they are all on their knees,'
An elder said as we sat in a flock
    By the embers in hearthside ease.

We pictured the meek mild creatures where
    They dwelt in their strawy pen,
Nor did it occur to one of us there
    To doubt they were kneeling then.

So fair a fancy few would weave
    In these years! Yet, I feel,
If someone said on Christmas Eve,
    'Come; see the oxen kneel

'In the lonely barton by yonder coomb
    Our childhood used to know,'
I should go with him in the gloom,
    Hoping it might be so.

THOMAS HARDY

SING A SONG OF SEASONS

AUTUMN FIRES

In the other gardens
    And all up the vale,
From the autumn bonfires
    See the smoke trail!

Pleasant summer over
    And all the summer flowers,
The red fire blazes,
    The grey smoke towers.

Sing a song of seasons!
    Something bright in all!
Flowers in the summer,
    Fires in the fall!

R. L. STEVENSON

'BREAD AND MILK FOR BREAKFAST'

Bread and milk for breakfast,
    And woollen frocks to wear,
And a crumb for robin redbreast
    On the cold days of the year.

CHRISTINA ROSSETTI

CUCKOO SONG

Tell it to the locked up trees,
Cuckoo, bring your song here!
Warrant, Act and Summons, please,
For Spring to pass along here!
Tell old Winter, if he doubt,
Tell him squat and square – a!
Old Woman!
Old Woman!
Old Woman's let the Cuckoo out
At Heffle Cuckoo Fair – a!

March has searched and April tried –
'Tisn't long to May now.
Not so far to Whitsuntide
And Cuckoo's come to stay now!
Hear the valiant fellow shout
Down the orchard bare – a!
Old Woman!
Old Woman!
Old Woman's let the Cuckoo out
At Heffle Cuckoo Fair – a!

When your heart is young and gay
And the season rules it –
Work your works and play your play
'Fore the Autumn cools it!
Kiss you turn and turn-about,
But, my lad, beware – a!
Old Woman!
Old Woman!
Old Woman's let the Cuckoo out
At Heffle Cuckoo Fair – a!

RUDYARD KIPLING

Rudyard Kipling writes, 'Spring begins in Southern England
on the 14th April, on which date the
Old Woman lets the Cuckoo out of her basket at
Heathfield Fair – locally known at Heffle Cuckoo Fair.'

'DEAR MARCH – COME IN – '

Dear March – Come in –
How glad I am –
I hoped for you before –
Put down your Hat –
You must have walked –
How out of Breath you are –
Dear March, how are you, and the Rest –
Did you leave Nature well –
Oh March, Come right up stairs with me –
I have so much to tell –

I got your Letter, and the Birds –
The Maples never knew that you were coming – till I called
I declare – how Red their Faces grew –
But March, forgive me – and
All those Hills you left for me to Hue –
There was no Purple suitable –
You took it all with you –

Who knocks? That April.
Lock the Door –
I will not be pursued –
He stayed away a Year to call
When I am occupied –
But trifles look so trivial
As soon as you have come

That Blame is just as dear as Praise
And Praise as Mere as Blame –

EMILY DICKINSON

IN THE FIELDS

Lord, when I look at lovely things which pass,
    Under old trees the shadows of young leaves
Dancing to please the wind along the grass,
    Or the gold stillness of the August sun on the August sheaves;
Can I believe there is a heavenlier world than this?
    And if there is
Will the strange heart of any everlasting thing
    Bring me these dreams that take my breath away?
They come at evening with the home-flying rooks and the scent of hay,
    Over the fields. They come in Spring.

CHARLOTTE MEW

SPRING

Sound the Flute!
Now it's mute.
Birds delight
Day and Night;
Nightingale
In the dale,
Lark in Sky,
Merrily,
Merrily, Merrily, to welcome in the Year.

Little Boy,
Full of joy;
Little Girl,
Sweet and small;
Cock does crow,
So do you;
Merry voice,
Infant noise,
Merrily, Merrily, to welcome in the Year.

Little Lamb,
Here I am;
Come and lick
My white neck;
Let me pull
Your soft Wool;
Let me kiss
Your soft face:
Merrily, Merrily, we welcome in the Year.

WILLIAM BLAKE

THE TREES ARE DOWN

— and he cried with a loud voice:
Hurt not the earth, neither the sea, nor the trees —
(Revelation)

They are cutting down the great plane-trees at the end of the gardens.
For days there has been the grate of the saw, the swish of the branches as
    they fall,
The crash of the trunks, the rustle of trodden leaves,
With the 'Whoops' and the 'Whoas,' the loud common talk, the loud
    common laughs of the men, above it all.

I remember one evening of a long past Spring
Turning in at a gate, getting out of a cart, and finding a large dead rat in
    the mud of the drive.
I remember thinking: alive or dead, a rat was a god-forsaken thing,
But at least, in May, that even a rat should be alive.

The week's work here is as good as done. There is just one bough
  On the roped bole, in the fine grey rain,
      Green and high
      And lonely against the sky.
        (Down now! —)
      And but for that,
      If an old dead rat
Did once, for a moment, unmake the Spring, I might never have thought of
    him again.

It is not for a moment the Spring is unmade today;
These were great trees, it was in them from root to stem:
When the men with the 'Whoops' and the 'Whoas' have carted the whole
    of the whispering loveliness away
Half the Spring, for me, will have gone with them.

It is going now, and my heart has been struck with the hearts of the planes;
Half my life it has beat with these, in the sun, in the rains,
   In the March wind, the May breeze,
In the great gales that came over to them across the roofs from the great seas.
   There was only a quiet rain when they were dying;
   They must have heard the sparrows flying,
And the small creeping creatures in the earth where they were lying –
   But I, all day, I heard an angel crying:
     'Hurt not the trees.'

CHARLOTTE MEW

DOMUS CAEDET ARBOREM
The House Will Fell the Tree

Ever since the great planes were murdered at the end of the gardens
The city, to me, at night has the look of a Spirit brooding crime;
As if the dark houses watching the trees from dark windows
   Were simply biding their time.

CHARLOTTE MEW

'THE LOPPED TREE IN TIME MAY GROW AGAIN'

The lopped tree in time may grow again,
Most naked plants renew both fruit and flower;
The sorriest wight may find release of pain,
The driest soil suck in some moistening shower.
Times go by turns, and chances change by course
From foul to fair, from better hap to worse.

The sea of fortune doth not ever flow,
She draws her favours to the lowest ebb
Her tides hath equal times to come and go,

Her loom doth weave the fine and coarsest web.
No joy so great but runneth to an end,
No hap so hard but may in fine amend.

Not always fall of leaf, nor ever spring,
No endless night, yet not eternal day;
The saddest birds a season find to sing,
The roughest storm a calm may soon allay.
Thus, with succeeding turns, God tempereth all,
That man may hope to rise, yet fear to fall.

A chance may win that by mischance was lost;
The net that holds no great, takes little fish;
In some things all, in all things none are crossed;
Few all they need, but none have all they wish.
Unmeddled joys here to no man befall;
Who least, hath some; who most, hath never all.

ROBERT SOUTHWELL

'LOVELIEST OF TREES, THE CHERRY NOW'

Loveliest of trees, the cherry now
Is hung with bloom along the bough,
And stands about the woodland ride
Wearing white for Eastertide.

Now, of my threescore years and ten,
Twenty will not come again,
And take from seventy springs a score,
It only leaves me fifty more.

And since to look at things in bloom
Fifty springs are little room,
About the woodlands I will go
To see the cherry hung with snow.

A. E. HOUSMAN

THE DAFFODILS

I wandered lonely as a cloud
That floats on high o'er vales and hills,
When all at once I saw a crowd,
A host, of golden daffodils;
Beside the lake, beneath the trees,
Fluttering and dancing in the breeze.

Continuous as the stars that shine
And twinkle on the milky way,
They stretched in never-ending line
Along the margin of a bay:
Ten thousand saw I at a glance,
Tossing their heads in sprightly dance.

The waves beside them danced; but they
Out-did the sparkling waves in glee:
A poet could not but be gay,
In such a jocund company:
I gazed – and gazed – but little thought
What wealth the show to me had brought:

For oft, when on my couch I lie
In vacant or in pensive mood,
They flash upon that inward eye
Which is the bliss of solitude;
And then my heart with pleasure fills,
And dances with the daffodils.

WILLIAM WORDSWORTH

jocund: cheerful

TO DAFFODILS

Fair Daffodils, we weep to see
  You haste away so soon;
As yet the early rising sun
  Has not attained his noon.
    Stay, stay,
   Until the hasting day
    Has run
   But to the even-song;
And, having prayed together, we
  Will go with you along.

We have short time to stay, as you,
  We have as short a spring;
As quick a growth to meet decay,
  As you, or anything.
    We die
   As your hours do, and dry
    Away,
   Like to the summer's rain;
Or as the pearls of morning's dew,
  Ne'er to be found again.

ROBERT HERRICK

THE WHEAT RIPENING

What time the wheat field tinges rusty brown
And barley bleaches in its mellow grey
Tis sweet some smooth mown baulk to wander down
Or cross the fields on footpaths narrow way
Just in the mealy light of waking day
As glittering dewdrops moist the maidens gown
And sparkling bounces from her nimble feet
Journeying to milking from the neighbouring town
Making life bright with song – and it is sweet
To mark the grazing herds and list the clown
Urge on his ploughing team with cheering calls
And merry shepherds whistling toils begun
And hoarse tongued bird boy whose unceasing calls
Join the larks ditty to the rising sun

JOHN CLARE

DAY-DREAMS

Broad August burns in milky skies,
   The world is blanched with hazy heat;
The vast green pasture, even, lies
   Too hot and bright for eyes and feet.

Amid the grassy levels rears
   The sycamore against the sun
The dark boughs of a hundred years,
   The emerald foliage of one.

Lulled in a dream of shade and sheen,
   Within the clement twilight thrown

By that great cloud of floating green,
   A horse is standing, still as stone.

He stirs nor head nor hoof, although
   The grass is fresh beneath the branch;
His tail alone swings to and fro
   In graceful curves from haunch to haunch.

He stands quite lost, indifferent
   To rack or pasture, trace or rein;
He feels the vaguely sweet content
   Of perfect sloth in limb and brain.

WILLIAM CANTON

HEAT

From plains that reel to southward, dim,
    The road runs by me white and bare;
Up the steep hill it seems to swim
    Beyond, and melt into the glare.
Upward half way, or it may be
    Nearer the summit, slowly steals
A hay-cart, moving dustily
    With idly clacking wheels.

By his cart's side the wagoner
    Is slouching slowly at his ease,
Half-hidden in the windless blur
    Of white dust puffing to his knees.
This wagon on the height above,
From sky to sky on either hand,
Is the sole thing that seems to move
    In all the heat-held land.

Beyond me in the fields the sun
    Soaks in the grass and hath his will;
I count the marguerites one by one;
    Even the buttercups are still.
On the brook yonder not a breath
Disturbs the spider or the midge.
The water-bugs draw close beneath
    The cool gloom of the bridge.

Where the far elm-tree shadows flood
    Dark patches in the burning grass,
The cows, each with her peaceful cud,
    Lie waiting for the heat to pass.
From somewhere on the slope near by
    Into the pale depth of the noon
A wandering thrush slides leisurely
    His thin revolving tune.

In intervals of dreams I hear
    The cricket from the droughty ground;
The grass-hoppers spin into mine ear
    A small innumerable sound.
I lift mine eyes sometimes to gaze:
    The burning sky-line blinds my sight:
The woods far off are blue with haze:
    The hills are drenched in light.

And yet to me not this or that
    Is always sharp or always sweet;
In the sloped shadow of my hat
    I lean at rest, and drain the heat;
Nay more, I think some blessèd power
    Hath brought me wandering idly here:
In the full furnace of this hour
    My thoughts grow keen and clear.

ARCHIBALD LAMPMAN

PODS POP AND GRIN

Strong strong sun, in that look
you have, lands ripen
fruits, trees, people.

Lands love the flame of your gaze.
Lands hide some warmth
of sun-eye for darkness.

All for you pods pop and grin.
Bananas hurry up and grow.
Coconut becomes water and oil.

Palm trees try to fly to you
but just dance everywhere.
Silk leaves of bamboo rustle wild.

And when rain finished falling
winds shake diamonds from branches
that again feel your eye.

Strong strong sun, in you
lands keep ripening
fruits, trees, people.

Birds go on tuning up
and don't care at all —
more blood berries are coming.

Your look strokes up all
summertime. We hear streams running.
You come back every day.

JAMES BERRY

CUT GRASS

Cut grass lies frail:
Brief is the breath
Mown stalks exhale.
Long, long the death

It dies in the white hours
Of young-leaved June
With chestnut flowers,
With hedges snowlike strewn,

White lilac bowed,
Lost lanes of Queen Anne's lace,
And that high-built cloud
Moving at summer's pace.

PHILIP LARKIN

'BLAZING IN GOLD'

Blazing in Gold and quenching in Purple
Leaping like Leopards to the Sky
Then at the feet of the old Horizon
Laying her spotted Face to die
Stooping as low as the Otter's Window
Touching the Roof and tinting the Barn
Kissing her Bonnet to the Meadow
And the Juggler of Day is gone

EMILY DICKINSON

'THE SUN AND FOG CONTESTED'

The Sun and Fog contested
The Government of Day –
The Sun took down his Yellow Whip
And drove the Fog away –

EMILY DICKINSON

THE RAINBOW

Rainbow, rainbow,
   Rin away hame;
Come again at Martinmas,
   When a' the corn's in.

TRADITIONAL

AUTUMN

A touch of cold in the Autumn night –
I walked abroad,
And saw the ruddy moon lean over a hedge
Like a red-faced farmer.
I did not stop to speak, but nodded,
And round about were the wistful stars
With white faces like town children.

T. E. HULME

WEATHERS

I

This is the weather the cuckoo likes,
   And so do I;
When showers betumble the chestnut spikes,
   And nestlings fly:
And the little brown nightingale bills his best,
And they sit outside at 'The Travellers' Rest',
And maids come forth sprig-muslin drest,
And citizens dream of the south and west,
   And so do I.

II

This is the weather the shepherd shuns,
   And so do I;
When beeches drip in browns and duns,
   And thresh, and ply;
And hill-hid tides throb, throe on throe,
And meadow rivulets overflow,
And drops on gate-bars hang in a row,
And rooks in families homeward go,
   And so do I.

THOMAS HARDY

TO AUTUMN

Season of mists and mellow fruitfulness!
　　Close bosom-friend of the maturing sun;
Conspiring with him how to load and bless
　　With fruit the vines that round the thatch-eves run;
To bend with apples the moss'd cottage-trees,
　　And fill all fruit with ripeness to the core;
　　　　To swell the gourd, and plump the hazel shells
　　With a sweet kernel; to set budding more,
And still more, later flowers for the bees,
Until they think warm days will never cease,
　　　　For Summer has o'er-brimm'd their clammy cells.

Who hath not seen thee oft amid thy store?
　　Sometimes whoever seeks abroad may find
Thee sitting careless on a granary floor,
　　Thy hair soft-lifted by the winnowing wind;
Or on a half-reap'd furrow sound asleep,
　　Drowsed with the fumes of poppies, while thy hook
　　　　Spares the next swath and all its twined flowers:
And sometimes like a gleaner thou dost keep
　　Steady thy laden head across a brook;
　　Or by a cyder-press, with patient look,
　　　　Thou watchest the last oozings hours by hours.

Where are the songs of Spring? Ay, where are they?
　　Think not of them, thou hast thy music too, –
While barred clouds bloom the soft-dying day,
　　And touch the stubble-plains with rosy hue;
Then in a wailful choir the small gnats mourn
　　Among the river sallows, borne aloft
　　　　Or sinking as the light wind lives or dies;
And full-grown lambs loud bleat from hilly bourn;
　　Hedge-crickets sing; and now with treble soft
　　The red-breast whistles from a garden-croft;
And gathering swallows twitter in the skies.

JOHN KEATS

BEECHWOODS AT KNOLE

How do I love you, beech-trees, in the autumn,
Your stone-grey columns a cathedral nave
Processional above the earth's brown glory!

I was a child, and loved the knurly tangle
Of roots that coiled above a scarp like serpents,
Where I might hide my treasure with the squirrels.

I was a child, and splashed my way in laughter
Through drifts of leaves, where underfoot the beech-nuts
Split with crisp crackle to my great rejoicing.

Red are the beechen slopes below Shock Tavern,
Red is the bracken on the sandy Furze-field,
Red are the stags and hinds by Bo-Pit Meadows,

The rutting stags that nightly through the beech-woods
Bell out their challenge, carrying their antlers
Proudly beneath the antlered autumn branches.

I was a child, and heard the red deer's challenge
Prowling and belling underneath my window,
Never a cry so haughty or so mournful.

VITA SACKVILLE-WEST

WILD IRON

Sea go dark, dark with wind,
Feet go heavy, heavy with sand,
Thoughts go wild, wild with the sound
Of iron on the old shed swinging, clanging:
Go dark, go heavy, go wild, go round,
  Dark with the wind,
  Heavy with the sand,
Wild with the iron that tears at the nail
And the foundering shriek of the gale.

ALLEN CURNOW

'WHO HAS SEEN THE WIND?'

Who has seen the wind?
  Neither I nor you:
But when the leaves hang trembling
  The wind is passing thro'.

Who has seen the wind?
  Neither you nor I:
But when the trees bow down their heads
  The wind is passing by.

CHRISTINA ROSSETTI

WINDY NIGHTS

Whenever the moon and stars are set,
  Whenever the wind is high,
All night long in the dark and wet,
  A man goes riding by.
Late in the night when the fires are out,
Why does he gallop and gallop about?

Whenever the trees are crying aloud,
  And ships are tossed at sea,
By, on the highway, low and loud,
  By at the gallop goes he.
By at the gallop he goes, and then
By he comes back at the gallop again.

R. L. STEVENSON

THE STORM

First there were two of us, then there were three of us,
Then there was one bird more,
Four of us – wild white sea-birds,
Treading the ocean floor;
And the *wind* rose, and the *sea* rose,
To the angry billows' roar –
With one of us – two of us – three of us – four of us
Sea-birds on the shore.

Soon there were five of us, soon there were nine of us,
And lo! in a trice sixteen!
And the yeasty surf curdled over the sands,
The gaunt grey rocks between;
And the tempest raved, and the lightning's fire
Struck blue on the spindrift hoar –
And on four of us – ay, and on four times four of us
Sea-birds on the shore.

And our sixteen waxed to thirty-two,
And they to past three score –
A wild, white welter of winnowing wings,
And ever more and more;
And the winds lulled, and the sea went down,
And the sun streamed out on high,
Gilding the pools and the spume and the spars
'Neath the vast blue deeps of the sky;

And the isles and the bright green headlands shone,
As they'd never shone before,
Mountains and valleys of silver cloud,
Wherein to swing, sweep, soar –
A host of screeching, scolding, scrabbling
Sea-birds on the shore –
A snowy, silent, sun-washed drift
Of sea-birds on the shore.

WALTER DE LA MARE

WINDY GAP

As I was going through Windy Gap
A hawk and a cloud hung over the map.

The land lay bare and the wind blew loud
And the hawk cried out from the heart of the cloud,

'Before I fold my wings in sleep
I'll pick the bones of your travelling sheep,

'For the leaves blow back and the wintry sun
Shows the tree's white skeleton.'

A magpie sat in the tree's high top
Singing a song on Windy Gap

That streamed far down to the plain below
Like a shaft of light from a high window.

From the bending tree he sang aloud,
And the sun shone out of the heart of the cloud

And it seemed to me as we travelled through
That my sheep were the notes that trumpet blew.

And so I sing this song of praise
For travelling sheep and blowing days.

DAVID CAMPBELL

ADDRESS TO A CHILD DURING A BOISTEROUS WINTER EVENING

What way does the Wind come? What way does he go?
He rides over the water, and over the snow,
Through wood and through vale; and o'er rocky height
Which the goat cannot climb, takes his sounding flight
    He tosses about in every bare tree,
    As, if you look up, you plainly may see;
But how he will come, and whither he goes,
There's never a scholar in England knows.

He will suddenly stop in a cunning nook,
And ring a sharp 'larum – but if you should look,
There's nothing to see but a cushion of snow
    Round as a pillow, and whiter than milk,
    And softer than if it were covered with silk.
Sometimes he'll hide in the cave of a rock,
Then whistle as shrill as the buzzard cock;
    Yet seek him – and what shall you find in the place?
    Nothing but silence and empty space;
Save, in a corner, a heap of dry leaves,
That he's left for a bed, to beggars or thieves.

As soon as 'tis daylight tomorrow, with me
You shall go to the orchard, and then you will see
That he has been there, and made a great rout,
And cracked the branches, and strewn them about;
    Heaven grant that he spare but that one upright twig
    That looked up at the sky so proud and big
All last summer, as well you know,
Studded with apples, a beautiful show!

Hark! over the roof he makes a pause,
And growls as if he would fix his claws
Right in the slates, and with a huge rattle
Drive them down, like men in a battle:
    But let him range round: he does us no harm,
    We build up the fire; we're snug and warm,
Untouched by his breath, see the candle shines bright,
And burns with a clear and steady light;
Books have we to read – but that half-stifled knell,
Alas, 'tis the sound of the eight o'clock bell.

Come now we'll to bed! And when we are there
He may work his own will, and what shall we care?
He may knock at the door – we'll not let him in;
May drive at the windows – we'll laugh at his din.
Let him seek his own home wherever it be;
Here's a cosy warm house for Edward and me.

DOROTHY WORDSWORTH

'larum: alarm

'O THOUGHT I!'

O thought I!
What a beautiful thing
God has made winter to be
by stripping the trees
and letting us see
their shapes and forms.
What a freedom does it seem
to give to the storms.

DOROTHY WORDSWORTH

*This is not a poem, but a piece of
prose from Dorothy Wordsworth's lovely
Grasmere Journal, broken into lines.*

THE HIGH HILLS

The high hills have a bitterness
Now they are not known
And memory is poor enough consolation
For the soul hopeless gone.
Up in the air there beech tangles wildly in the wind –
That I can imagine
But the speed, the swiftness, walking into clarity,
Like last year's bryony are gone.

IVOR GURNEY

'AN OCTOBER ROBIN . . .'

An October robin kept
Stringing its song
On gossamer that snapped.
The weir-pool hung
Lit with honey leaves.
Ploughed hills crisp as loaves

In the high morning.
I waded the river's way
Body and ear leaning
For whatever the world might say
Of the word in her womb
Curled unborn and dumb.

Still as the heron
I let the world grow near
With a ghostly salmon
Hanging in thin air
So real it was holy
And watching seemed to kneel.

And there I saw the vixen
Coiled on her bank porch.
Her paws were bloody sticks.
Ears on guard for her searchers
She had risked a sleep
And misjudged how deep.

TED HUGHES

'PLEASE TO REMEMBER'

Here am I,
A poor old Guy:
Legs in a bonfire,
Head in the sky;

Shoeless my toes,
Wild stars behind,
Smoke in my nose,
And my eye-peeps blind;

Old hat, old straw –
In this disgrace;
While the wildfire gleams
On a mask for face.

Ay, all I am made of
Only trash is;
And soon – soon,
Will be dust and ashes.

WALTER DE LA MARE

*On the fifth of November, British children
burn effigies of Guy Fawkes,
who plotted to burn down Parliament.*

'THERE'S A CERTAIN SLANT OF LIGHT'

There's a certain Slant of light,
Winter Afternoons –
That oppresses, like the Heft
Of Cathedral Tunes –

Heavenly Hurt, it gives us –
We can find no scar,
But internal difference,
Where the Meanings, are –

None may teach it – Any –
'Tis the Seal Despair –
An imperial affliction
Sent us of the Air –

When it comes, the Landscape listens –
Shadows – hold their breath –
When it goes, 'tis like the Distance
On the look of Death –

EMILY DICKINSON

SNOW

In the gloom of whiteness,
In the great silence of snow,
A child was sighing
And bitterly saying: 'Oh,
They have killed a white bird up there on her nest,
The down is fluttering from her breast!'
And still it fell through that dusky brightness
On the child crying for the bird of the snow.

EDWARD THOMAS

NOW WINTER NIGHTS ENLARGE

Now winter nights enlarge
   The number of their hours,
And clouds their storms discharge
   Upon the airy towers.
Let now the chimneys blaze,
   And cups o'erflow with wine;
Let well-tuned words amaze
   With harmony divine.
Now yellow waxen lights
   Shall wait on honey Love,
While youthful revels, masks, and courtly sights
   Sleep's leaden spells remove.

This time doth well dispense
   With lovers' long discourse.
Much speech hath some defence
   Though beauty no remorse.
All do not all things well:
   Some measures comely tread,
Some knotted riddles tell,
   Some poems smoothly read.
The Summer hath his joys,
   And Winter his delights.
Though Love and all his pleasures are but toys,
   They shorten tedious nights.

THOMAS CAMPION

STOPPING BY WOODS ON A SNOWY EVENING

Whose woods these are I think I know.
His house is in the village though;
He will not see me stopping here
To watch his woods fill up with snow.

My little horse must think it queer
To stop without a farmhouse near
Between the woods and frozen lake
The darkest evening of the year.

He gives his harness bells a shake
To ask if there is some mistake.
The only other sound's the sweep
Of easy wind and downy flake.

The woods are lovely, dark and deep,
But I have promises to keep,
And miles to go before I sleep,
And miles to go before I sleep.

ROBERT FROST

THAW

Over the land freckled with snow half-thawed
The speculating rooks at their nests cawed
And saw from elm-tops, delicate as flower of grass,
What we below could not see, winter pass.

EDWARD THOMAS

SUDDEN THAW

When day dawned with unusual light,
Hedges in snow stood half their height
And in the white-paved village street
Children were walking without feet.

But now by their own breath kept warm
Muck-heaps are naked at the farm
And even through the shrinking snow
Dead bents and thistles start to grow.

ANDREW YOUNG

SONG BY AN OLD SHEPHERD

When silver snow decks Sylvio's clothes
And jewel hangs at shepherd's nose,
We can abide life's pelting storm
That makes our limbs quake, if our hearts be warm.

Whilst Virtue is our walking-staff
And Truth a lantern to our path,
We can abide life's pelting storm
That makes our limbs quake, if our hearts be warm.

Blow, boisterous wind, stern winter frown,
Innocence is a winter's gown;
So clad, we'll abide life's pelting storm
That makes our limbs quake, if our hearts be warm.

WILLIAM BLAKE

SNOW FALLING

A white newspaper sky
Ruled out for writing
With telephone wires
For the lines!
A sky full of snow flakes!

The snow looks like dust
Coming down;
Snow-dust,
Diving round and round
And down
All the little snow flakes
Are falling to pieces

So small that they are blown
The way of the breeze
Before they land.
Snow on the seat
Looks like sugar sprinkled.
Large flakes fall softly
And slowly to the ground.

A blackbird, with orange beak
Is sitting on the path
Feeling the snow.
Birds at a distance
Look like little round balls,
Black balls rolling along the sky.

Now the snow is coming quicker.
Snow flakes play 'Follow-my-leader',
Running round and round in a ring
Like a circus.
Now slowly
Like strings of cotton
Threaded to round snow buttons.

GILLIAN HUGHES

Gillian Hughes wrote this poem at the age of six

CHRISTMAS SONG

The trees are all bare not a leaf to be seen
And the meadows their beauty have lost.
Now winter has come and 'tis cold for man and beast,
And the streams they are,
And the streams they are all fast bound down with frost.

'Twas down in the farmyard where the oxen feed on straw,
They send forth their breath like the steam.
Sweet Betsy the milkmaid now quickly she must go,
For flakes of ice she finds,
For flakes of ice she finds a-floating on her cream.

'Tis now all the small birds to the barn-door fly for food
And gently they rest on the spray.
A-down the plantation the hares do search for food,
And lift their footsteps sure,
Lift their footsteps sure for fear they do betray.

Now Christmas is come and our song is almost done
For we soon shall have the turn of the year.
So fill up your glasses and let your health go round,
For I wish you all,
For I wish you all a joyful New Year.

TRADITIONAL

CHILDREN

IF YOU DARE TO THINK

WARNING TO CHILDREN

Children, if you dare to think
Of the greatness, rareness, muchness,
Fewness of this precious only
Endless world in which you say
You live, you think of things like this:
Blocks of slate enclosing dappled
Red and green, enclosing tawny
Yellow nets, enclosing white
And black acres of dominoes,
Where a neat brown paper parcel
Tempts you to untie the string.
In the parcel a small island,
On the island a large tree,
On the tree a husky fruit.
Strip the husk and pare the rind off:
In the kernel you will see
Blocks of slate enclosed by dappled
Red and green, enclosed by tawny
Yellow nets, enclosed by white

And black acres of dominoes,
Where the same brown paper parcel –
Children, leave the string untied!
For who dares undo the parcel
Finds himself at once inside it,
On the island, in the fruit,
Blocks of slate about his head,
Finds himself enclosed by dappled
Green and red, enclosed by yellow
Tawny nets, enclosed by black
And white acres of dominoes,
With the same brown paper parcel
Still untied upon his knee.
And, if he then should dare to think
Of the fewness, muchness, rareness,
Greatness of this endless only
Precious world in which he says
He lives – he then unties the string.

ROBERT GRAVES

LEISURE

What is this life if, full of care,
We have no time to stand and stare.

No time to stand beneath the boughs
And stare as long as sheep or cows.

No time to see, when woods we pass,
Where squirrels hide their nuts in grass.

No time to see, in broad daylight,
Streams full of stars like skies at night.

No time to turn at Beauty's glance,
And watch her feet, how they can dance.

No time to wait till her mouth can
Enrich that smile her eyes began.

A poor life this if, full of care,
We have no time to stand and stare.

W. H. DAVIES

COCK-CROW

Out of the wood of thoughts that grows by night
To be cut down by the sharp axe of light, –
Out of the night, two cocks together crow,
Cleaving the darkness with a silver blow:
And bright before my eyes twin trumpeters stand,
Heralds of splendour, one at either hand,
Each facing each as in a coat of arms:
The milkers lace their boots up at the farms.

EDWARD THOMAS

'A THING OF BEAUTY'

A thing of beauty is a joy for ever:
Its loveliness increases; it will never
Pass into nothingness, but still will keep
A bower quiet for us, and a sleep
Full of sweet dreams, and health, and quiet breathing.
Therefore, on every morrow, are we wreathing
A flowery band to bind us to the earth,
Spite of despondence, of the inhuman dearth
Of noble natures, of the gloomy days,
Of all the unhealthy and o'er-darkened ways
Made for our searching: yes, in spite of all,
Some shape of beauty moves away the pall
From our dark spirits. Such the sun, the moon,
Trees old and young, sprouting a shady boon
For simple sheep; and such are daffodils
With the green world they live in; and clear rills
That for themselves a cooling covert make
'Gainst the hot season; the mid-forest brake,
Rich with a sprinkling of fair musk-rose blooms:
And such too is the grandeur of the dooms
We have imagined for the mighty dead;
All lovely tales that we have heard or read:
An endless fountain of immortal drink,
Pouring unto us from the heaven's brink.

JOHN KEATS

THE LAKE ISLE OF INNISFREE

I will arise and go now, and go to Innisfree,
And a small cabin build there, of clay and wattles made:
Nine bean-rows will I have there, a hive for the honey-bee,
And live alone in the bee-loud glade.

And I shall have some peace there, for peace comes dropping slow,
Dropping from the veils of the morning to where the cricket sings;
There midnight's all a glimmer, and noon a purple glow,
And evening full of the linnet's wings.

I will arise and go now, for always night and day
I hear lake water lapping with low sounds by the shore;
While I stand on the roadway, or on the pavements grey,
I hear it in the deep heart's core.

W. B. YEATS

PROPHECY

I shall lie hidden in a hut
  In the middle of an alder wood,
With the back door blind and bolted shut,
  And the front door locked for good.

I shall lie folded like a saint,
  Lapped in a scented linen sheet,
On a bedstead striped with bright-blue paint,
  Narrow and cold and neat.

The midnight will be glassy black
  Behind the panes, with wind about
To set his mouth against a crack
  And blow the candle out.

ELINOR WYLIE

'WHITE IN THE MOON . . .'

White in the moon the long road lies,
  The moon stands blank above;
White in the moon the long road lies
  That leads me from my love.

Still hangs the hedge without a gust,
  Still, still the shadows stay:
My feet upon the moonlit dust
  Pursue the ceaseless way.

The world is round, so travellers tell,
  And straight though reach the track,
Trudge on, trudge on, 'twill all be well,
  The way will guide one back.

But ere the circle homeward hies
  Far, far must it remove:
White in the moon the long road lies
  That leads me from my love.

A. E. HOUSMAN

'BEFORE THE BEGINNING OF YEARS'

Before the beginning of years
   There came to the making of man
Time, with a gift of tears;
   Grief, with a glass that ran;
Pleasure, with pain for leaven;
   Summer, with flowers that fell;
Remembrance fallen from heaven,
   And madness risen from hell;
Strength without hands to smite;
   Love that endures for a breath:
Night, the shadow of light,
   And life, the shadow of death.

And the high gods took in hand
   Fire, and the falling of tears,
And a measure of sliding sand
   From under the feet of the years;
And froth and drift of the sea;
   And dust of the labouring earth;
And bodies of things to be
   In the houses of death and of birth;
And wrought with weeping and laughter,
   And fashioned with loathing and love,
With life before and after
   And death beneath and above,

For a day and a night and a morrow,
   That his strength might endure for a span
With travail and heavy sorrow,
   The holy spirit of man.

From the winds of the north and the south
   They gathered as unto strife;
They breathed upon his mouth,
   They filled his body with life;
Eyesight and speech they wrought
   For the veils of the soul therein,
A time for labour and thought,
   A time to serve and to sin;
They gave him light in his ways,
   And love, and a space for delight,
And beauty and length of days,
   And night, and sleep in the night.
His speech is a burning fire;
   With his lips he travaileth;
In his heart is a blind desire,
   In his eyes foreknowledge of death;
He weaves, and is clothed with derision;
   Sows, and he shall not reap;
His life is a watch or a vision
   Between a sleep and a sleep.

ALGERNON CHARLES SWINBURNE

'I THANK YOU GOD . . .'

i thank You God for most this amazing
day: for leaping greenly spirits of trees
and a blue true dream of sky; and for everything
which is natural which is infinite which is yes

(i who have died am alive again today,
and this is the sun's birthday; this is the birth
day of life and of love and wings: and of the gay
great happening illimitably earth)

how should tasting touching hearing seeing
breathing any – lifted from the no
of all nothing – human merely being
doubt unimaginable You?

(now the ears of my ears awake and
now the eyes of my eyes are opened)

E. E. CUMMINGS

PIED BEAUTY

Glory be to God for dappled things –
    For skies of couple-colour as a brinded cow;
      For rose-moles all in stipple upon trout that swim;
Fresh-firecoal chestnut-falls; finches' wings;
    Landscape plotted and pieced – fold, fallow, and plough;
      And áll trádes, their gear and tackle and trim.

All things counter, original, spare, strange;
    Whatever is fickle, freckled (who knows how?)
      With swift, slow; sweet, sour; adazzle, dim;
He fathers-forth whose beauty is past change:
      Praise him.

GERARD MANLEY HOPKINS

'CITIES AND THRONES AND POWERS'

Cities and Thrones and Powers
   Stand in Time's eye,
Almost as long as flowers,
   Which daily die:
But, as new buds put forth
   To glad new men,
Out of the spent and unconsidered Earth
   The Cities rise again.

This season's Daffodil,
   She never hears
What change, what chance, what chill,
   Cut down last year's;
But with bold countenance,
   And knowledge small,
Esteems her seven days' continuance
   To be perpetual.

So Time that is o'er-kind
   To all that be,
Ordains us e'en as blind,
   As bold as she:
That in our very death,
   And burial sure,
Shadow to shadow, well persuaded, saith,
   'See how our works endure!'

RUDYARD KIPLING

OZYMANDIAS

I met a traveller from an antique land
Who said: Two vast and trunkless legs of stone
Stand in the desert. Near them, on the sand,
Half sunk, a shattered visage lies, whose frown,
And wrinkled lip, and sneer of cold command,
Tell that its sculptor well those passions read
Which yet survive (stamped on these lifeless things),
The hand that mocked them and the heart that fed;
And on the pedestal these words appear:
'My name is Ozymandias, king of kings;
Look on my works, ye Mighty, and despair!'
Nothing beside remains. Round the decay
Of that colossal wreck, boundless and bare,
The lone and level sands stretch far away.

PERCY BYSSHE SHELLEY

'EVEN SUCH IS TIME . . .'

Even such is Time, that takes in trust
  Our youth, our joys, our all we have,
And pays us but with earth and dust;
  Who, in the dark and silent grave,
When we have wandered all our ways,
Shuts up the story of our days;
But from this earth, this grave, this dust,
My God shall raise me up, I trust.

SIR WALTER RALEGH

This verse was found in
Sir Walter's Bible after his death.

'A WORD IS DEAD'

A word is dead
When it is said,
Some say.
I say it just
Begins to live
That day.

EMILY DICKINSON

'HE WHO BINDS TO HIMSELF A JOY'

He who binds to himself a joy
Doth the winged life destroy;
But he who kisses the joy as it flies
Lives in Eternity's sun rise.

WILLIAM BLAKE

FANTASY OF AN AFRICAN BOY

Such a peculiar lot
we are, we people
without money, in daylong
yearlong sunlight, knowing
money is somewhere, somewhere,

Everybody says it's a big
bigger brain bother now,
money. Such millions and millions
of us don't manage at all
without it, like war going on.

And we can't eat it. Yet
without it our heads alone
stay big, as lots and lots do,
coming from nowhere joyful,
going nowhere happy.

We can't drink it up. Yet
without it we shrivel when small
and stop forever
where we stopped,
as lots and lots do.

We can't read money for books.
Yet without it we don't
read, don't write numbers,
don't open gates in other countries,
as lots and lots never do.

We can't use money to bandage
sores, can't pound it
to powder for sick eyes
and sick bellies. Yet without
it, flesh melts from our bones.

Such walled-round gentlemen
overseas minding money! Such
bigtime gentlemen, body guarded
because of too much respect
and too many wishes on them.

Too many wishes, everywhere,
wanting them to let go
magic of money, and let it fly
away, everywhere, day and night,
just like dropped leaves in wind!

JAMES BERRY

HUNGER

I come among the peoples like a shadow.
I sit down by each man's side.

None sees me, but they look on one another,
And know that I am there.

My silence is like the silence of the tide
That buries the playground of children;

Like the deepening of frost in the slow night,
When birds are dead in the morning.

Armies trample, invade, destroy,
With guns roaring from earth and air.

I am more terrible than armies,
I am more feared than the cannon.

Kings and chancellors give commands;
I give no command to any;

But I am listened to more than kings
And more than passionate orators.

I unswear words, and undo deeds.
Naked things know me.

I am first and last to be felt of the living.
I am Hunger.

LAURENCE BINYON

ABOU BEN ADHEM

Abou Ben Adhem (may his tribe increase!)
Awoke one night from a deep dream of peace,
And saw, within the moonlight in his room,
Making it rich, and like a lily in bloom,
An angel writing in a book of gold: —
Exceeding peace had made Ben Adhem bold,
And to the presence in the room he said,
'What writest thou?' — The vision raised its head,
And with a look made of all sweet accord,
Answered, 'The names of those who love the Lord.'
'And is mine one?' said Abou. 'Nay, not so,'
Replied the angel. Abou spoke more low,
But cheerly still; and said, 'I pray thee then,
Write me as one that loves his fellow-men.'

The angel wrote, and vanished. The next night
It came again with a great wakening light,
And showed the names whom love of God had blessed,
And lo! Ben Adhem's name led all the rest.

LEIGH HUNT

SONG

I hid my love when young while I
Couldn't bear the buzzing of a flye
I hid my love to my despite
Till I could not bear to look at light
I dare not gaze upon her face
But left her memory in each place
Where ere I saw a wild flower lye
I kissed and bade my love good bye

I met her in the greenest dells
Where dew drops pearl the wood blue bells
The lost breeze kissed her bright blue eye
The bee kissed and went singing bye
A sun beam found a passage there
A gold chain round her neck so fair
As secret as the wild bees song
She lay there all the summer long

I hid my love in field and town
Till e'en the breeze would knock me down
The Bees seemed singing ballads o'er
The flyes buzz turned a Lions roar
And even silence found a tongue
To haunt me all the summer long
The riddle nature could not prove
Was nothing else but secret love

JOHN CLARE

'DONT-CARE DIDN'T CARE'

Dont-care didn't care;
　　Dont-care was wild.
Dont-care stole plum and pear
　　Like any beggar's child.

Dont-care was made to care,
　　Dont-care was hung:
Dont-care was put in the pot
　　And boiled till he was done.

TRADITIONAL

A POISON TREE

I was angry with my friend:
I told my wrath, my wrath did end.
I was angry with my foe:
I told it not, my wrath did grow.

And I water'd it in fears,
Night and morning with my tears;
And I sunned it with smiles,
And with soft deceitful wiles.

And it grew both day and night,
Till it bore an apple bright;
And my foe beheld it shine,
And he knew that it was mine,

And into my garden stole
When the night had veil'd the pole:
In the morning glad I see
My foe outstretch'd beneath the tree.

WILLIAM BLAKE

ANGER'S FREEING POWER

I had a dream three walls stood up wherein a raven bird
Against the walls did beat himself and was not this absurd?

For sun and rain beat in that cell that had its fourth wall free
And daily blew the summer shower and the rain came presently

And all the pretty summer time and all the winter too
That foolish bird did beat himself till he was black and blue

Rouse up, rouse up, my raven bird, fly by the open wall
You make a prison of a place that is not one at all.

I took my raven by the hand, Oh come, I said, my Raven,
And I will take you by the hand and you shall fly to heaven.

But oh he sobbed and oh he sighed and in a fit he lay
Until two fellow ravens came and stood outside to say:

You wretched bird, conceited lump
You well deserve to pine and thump.

See now a wonder, mark it well
My bird rears up in angry spell,

Oh do I then? he says, and careless flies
O'er flattened wall at once to heaven's skies.

And in my dream I watched him go
And I was glad, I loved him so,

Yet when I woke my eyes were wet
To think Love had not freed my pet

Anger it was that won him hence
As only Anger taught him sense.

Often my tears fall in a shower
Because of Anger's freeing power.

STEVIE SMITH

THE JEELY PIECE SONG

I'm a skyscraper wean; I live on the nineteenth flair,
But I'm no gaun oot tae play ony mair,
'Cause since we moved tae Castlemilk, I'm wastin' away
'Cause I'm gettin' wan meal less every day:

Ch.   *Oh ye cannae fling pieces oot a twenty storey flat,*
Seven hundred hungry weans'll testify to that.
If it's butter, cheese or jeely, if the breid is plain or pan,
The odds against it reaching earth are ninety-nine tae wan.

On the first day ma maw flung oot a daud o' Hovis broon;
It came skytin' oot the windae and went up insteid o' doon.
Noo every twenty-seven hoors it comes back intae sight
'Cause ma piece went intae orbit and became a satellite.

On the second day ma maw flung me a piece oot wance again.
It went and hut the pilot in a fast low-flying plane.
He scraped it aff his goggles, shouting through the intercom,
'The Clydeside Reds huv goat me wi' a breid-an-jeely bomb.'

On the third day ma maw thought she would try another throw.
The Salvation Army band was staunin' doon below.
'Onward, Christian Soldiers' was the piece they should've played
But the oompah man was playing a piece an' marmalade.

We've wrote away to Oxfam to try an' get some aid,
An' a' the weans in Castlemilk have formed a 'piece brigade'.
We're gonnae march to George's Square demanding civil rights
Like nae mair hooses ower piece-flinging height.

ADAM McNAUGHTAN

A jeely piece is a jam sandwich. This is the song of a child ('wean') moved from a house in central Glasgow, Scotland, to a high-rise housing project.

THE GLOG-HOLE

I ken a glog-hole
    That looks at the sky
As much as to say
    I'm as deep as you're high!

HUGH MACDIARMID

ken: know
glog-hole: dark hole

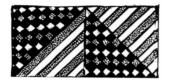

'I, TOO, SING AMERICA'

I, too, sing America.

I am the darker brother.
They send me to eat in the kitchen
When company comes,
But I laugh,
And eat well,
And grow strong.

Tomorrow,
I'll sit at the table
When company comes.
Nobody'll dare
Say to me,
'Eat in the kitchen,'
Then.

Besides,
They'll see how beautiful I am
And be ashamed –

I, too, am America.

LANGSTON HUGHES

NONE IS THE SAME AS ANOTHER

None is the same as another,
O none is the same.

That none is the same as another
is matter for crying
since never again will you see
that one, once gone.

In their brown hoods
the pilgrims are crossing the land
and many will look the same
but all are different

and their ideas fly to them
on accidental winds
perching awhile in their minds
from different valleys.

None is the same as another,
O none is the same.

And that none is the same is not
a matter for crying.

Stranger, I take your hand,
O changing stranger.

IAIN CRICHTON SMITH

AS YOU CAME FROM THE HOLY LAND

As you came from the holy land
  Of Walsingham
Met you not with my true love
  By the way as you came?

How shall I know your true love
  That have met many one
As I went to the holy land
  That have come, that have gone?

She is neither white nor brown
  But as the heavens fair,
There is none hath a form so divine
  In the earth or the air.

Such an one did I meet, good Sir,
  Such an angelic face,
Who like a queen, like a nymph, did appear
  By her gait, by her grace.

She hath left me here all alone,
  All alone as unknown,
Who sometimes did me lead with herself,
  And me loved as her own.

What's the cause that she leaves you alone
  And a new way doth take;
Who loved you once as her own
  And her joy did you make?

I have loved her all my youth,
  But now old, as you see,
Love likes not the falling fruit
  From the withered tree.

Know that love is a careless child
  And forgets promise past,
He is blind, he is deaf when he list
  And in faith never fast.

His desire is a dureless content
  And a trustless joy,
He is won with a world of despair
  And lost with a toy.

Of women-kind such indeed is the love,
  Or the word love abused,
Under which many childish desires
  And conceits are excused.

But true love is a durable fire
  In the mind ever burning;
Never sick, never old, never dead,
  From itself never turning.

                    SIR WALTER RALEGH

Walsingham Abbey in Norfolk, England, was a place of pilgrimage. Dureless: transient, not lasting.

THE BEAUTIFUL

Three things there are more beautiful
  Than any man could wish to see:
The first, it is a full-rigged ship
  Sailing with all her sails set free;
The second, when the wind and sun
  Are playing in a field of corn;
The third, a woman, young and fair,
  Showing her child before it is born.

W. H. DAVIES

THE ROAD NOT TAKEN

Two roads diverged in a yellow wood,
And sorry I could not travel both
And be one traveller, long I stood
And looked down one as far as I could
To where it bent in the undergrowth;

Then took the other, as just as fair,
And having perhaps the better claim,
Because it was grassy and wanted wear;
Though as for that the passing there
Had worn them really about the same,

And both that morning equally lay
In leaves no step had trodden black.
Oh, I kept the first for another day!
Yet knowing how way leads on to way,
I doubted if I should ever come back.

I shall be telling this with a sigh
Somewhere ages and ages hence:
Two roads diverged in a wood, and I —
I took the one less travelled by,
And that has made all the difference.

ROBERT FROST

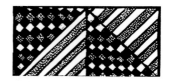

THIS IS THE KEY

This is the Key of the Kingdom
In that Kingdom is a city;
In that city is a town;
In that town there is a street;
In that street there winds a lane;
In that lane there is a yard;
In that yard there is a house;
In that house there waits a room;
In that room an empty bed;
And on that bed a basket —
A Basket of Sweet Flowers:
  Of Flowers, of Flowers;
  A Basket of Sweet Flowers.

Flowers in a Basket;
Basket on the bed;
Bed in the chamber;
Chamber in the house;
House in the weedy yard;
Yard in the winding lane;
Lane in the broad street;
Street in the high town;
Town in the city;
City in the Kingdom —
This is the Key of the Kingdom.
  Of the Kingdom this is the Key.

TRADITIONAL

'THE BRAIN – IS WIDER THAN THE SKY –'

The Brain – is wider than the Sky –
For – put them side by side –
The one the other will contain
With ease – and You – beside –

The Brain is deeper than the sea –
For – hold them – Blue to Blue –
The one the other will absorb –
As Sponges – Buckets – do –

The Brain is just the weight of God –
For – Heft them – Pound for Pound –
And they will differ – if they do –
As Syllable from Sound –

EMILY DICKINSON

GENERATIONS

The ploughed field and the fallow field
They sang a prudent song to me:
We bide all year and take our yield
Or barrenness as case may be.

What time or tide may bring to pass
Is nothing of our reckoning,
Power was before our making was
That had in brooding thought its spring.

We bide our fate as best betides
What ends the tale may prove the first.
Stars know as truly of their guides
As we the truth of best or worst.

IVOR GURNEY

MERLIN AND THE GLEAM

O young Mariner,
You from the haven
Under the sea-cliff,
You that are watching
The gray Magician
With eyes of wonder,
I am Merlin,
And *I* am dying,
I am Merlin
Who follow The Gleam.

Mighty the Wizard
Who found me at sunrise
Sleeping, and woke me!
And learned me Magic!
Great the Master,
And sweet the Magic,
When over the valley,
In early summers,
Over the mountain,
On human faces,
And all around me,
Moving to melody,
Floated The Gleam.

Once at the croak of a Raven who crost it,
A barbarous people,
Blind to the magic,
And deaf to the melody,
Snarl'd at and cursed me.
A demon vext me,
The light retreated,
The landskip darkened,
The melody deadened,
The Master whispered
'Follow The Gleam.'

Then to the melody,
Over a wilderness

Gliding, and glancing at
Elf of the woodland,
Gnome of the cavern,
Griffin and Giant,
And dancing of Fairies
In desolate hollows,
And wraiths of the mountain,
And rolling of dragons
By warble of water,
Or cataract music
Of falling torrents,
Flitted The Gleam.

Down from the mountain
And over the level,
And streaming and shining on
Silent river,
Silvery willow,
Pasture and plowland,
Innocent maidens,
Garrulous children,
Homestead and harvest,
Reaper and gleaner,
And rough-ruddy faces
Of lowly labour,
Slided The Gleam –

Then, with a melody
Stronger and statelier,
Led me at length
To the city and palace

Of Arthur the king;
Touched at the golden
Cross of the churches,
Flashed on the Tournament,
Flickered and bickered
From helmet to helmet,
And last on the forehead
Of Arthur the blameless
Rested The Gleam.

Clouds and darkness
Closed upon Camelot;
Arthur had vanished
I knew not whither,
The king who loved me,
And cannot die;
For out of the darkness
Silent and slowly
The Gleam, that had waned to a wintry glimmer
On icy fallow
And faded forest,
Drew to the valley
Named of the shadow,
And slowly brightening
Out of the glimmer,
And slowly moving again to a melody
Yearningly tender,
Fell on the shadow,
No longer a shadow,
But clothed with The Gleam.

And broader and brighter
The Gleam flying onward,
Wed to the melody,
Sang thro' the world;
And slower and fainter,
Old and weary,
But eager to follow,
I saw, whenever
In passing it glanced upon
Hamlet or city,
That under the Crosses
The dead man's garden,
The mortal hillock
Would break into blossom;
And so to the land's
Last limit I came –
And can no longer,
But die rejoicing,
For thro' the Magic
Of Him the Mighty,
Who taught me in childhood,
There on the border
Of boundless Ocean,
And all but in Heaven
Hovers the Gleam.

Not of the sunlight,
Not of the moonlight,
Not of the starlight!
O young Mariner,
Down to the haven,
Call your companions,
Launch your vessel,
And crowd your canvas,
And, ere it vanishes
Over the margin,
After it, follow it,
Follow The Gleam.

ALFRED TENNYSON

THE RAINBOW

Even the rainbow has a body
made of the drizzling rain
and is an architecture of glistening atoms
built up, built up
yet you can't lay your hand on it,
nay, nor even your mind.

D. H. LAWRENCE

THE RAINBOW

I saw the lovely arch
Of Rainbow span the sky,
The gold sun burning
As the rain swept by.

In bright-ringed solitude
The showery foliage shone
One lovely moment,
And the Bow was gone.

WALTER DE LA MARE

'MY HEART LEAPS UP'

My heart leaps up when I behold
    A rainbow in the sky:
So was it when my life began;
So is it now I am a man;
So be it when I shall grow old,
    Or let me die!
The Child is father of the Man;
And I could wish my days to be
Bound each to each by natural piety.

WILLIAM WORDSWORTH

'THE CHILD IS FATHER TO THE MAN'

'The child is father to the man.'
How can he be? The words are wild.
Suck any sense from that who can:
'The child is father to the man.'
No; what the poet did write ran,
'The man is father to the child.'
'The child is father to the man!'
How *can* he be? The words are wild.

GERARD MANLEY HOPKINS

'WHAT ARE HEAVY?'

What are heavy? sea-sand and sorrow:
What are brief? today and tomorrow:
What are frail? Spring blossoms and youth:
What are deep? the ocean and truth.

CHRISTINA ROSSETTI

'SAY NOT THE STRUGGLE NOUGHT AVAILETH . . .'

Say not the struggle nought availeth,
  The labour and the wounds are vain,
The enemy faints not, nor faileth,
  And as things have been they remain.

If hopes were dupes, fears may be liars;
  It may be, in yon smoke concealed,
Your comrades chase e'en now the fliers,
  And, but for you, possess the field.

For while the tired waves, vainly breaking,
  Seem here no painful inch to gain,
Far back, through creeks and inlets making,
  Comes silent, flooding in, the main.

And not by eastern windows only,
  When daylight comes, comes in the light;
In front, the sun climbs slow, how slowly,
  But westward, look, the land is bright!

ARTHUR HUGH CLOUGH

'IN THIS SHORT LIFE'

In this short Life
That only lasts an hour
How much – how little – is
Within our power

EMILY DICKINSON

PERSONAL

In an envelope marked:
Personal
God addressed me a letter.
In an envelope marked:
Personal
I have given my answer.

LANGSTON HUGHES

'WHERE LIES THE LAND . . .'

Where lies the land to which the ship would go?
Far, far ahead, is all her seamen know.
And where the land she travels from? Away,
Far, far behind, is all that they can say.

On sunny noons upon the deck's smooth face,
Linked arm in arm, how pleasant here to pace!
Or, o'er the stern reclining, watch below
The foaming wake far widening as we go.

On stormy nights when wild north-westers rave,
How proud a thing to fight with wind and wave!
The dripping sailor on the reeling mast
Exults to bear, and scorns to wish it past.

Where lies the land to which the ship would go?
Far, far ahead, is all her seamen know.
And where the land she travels from? Away,
Far, far behind, is all that they can say.

ARTHUR HUGH CLOUGH

I AM THE GREAT SUN

From a Normandy crucifix of 1632

I am the great sun, but you do not see me,
   I am your husband, but you turn away.
I am the captive, but you do not free me,
   I am the captain you will not obey.

I am the truth, but you will not believe me,
   I am the city where you will not stay,
I am your wife, your child, but you will leave me,
   I am that God to whom you will not pray.

I am your counsel, but you do not hear me,
   I am the lover whom you will betray,
I am the victor, but you do not cheer me,
   I am the holy dove whom you will slay.

I am your life, but if you will not name me,
Seal up your soul with tears, and never blame me.

CHARLES CAUSLEY

'I TOOK ONE DRAUGHT OF LIFE – '

I took one Draught of Life –
I'll tell you what I paid –
Precisely an existence –
The market price, they said.

They weighed me, Dust by Dust –
They balanced Film with Film,
They handed me my Being's worth –
A single Dram of Heaven!

EMILY DICKINSON

From AUGURIES OF INNOCENCE

To see a World in a Grain of Sand
And a Heaven in a Wild Flower,
Hold Infinity in the palm of your hand
And Eternity in an hour.

WILLIAM BLAKE

ONCE UPON A TIME

THE CATARACT OF LODORE

'How does the Water
Come down at Lodore?'
My little boy asked me
Thus, once on a time;
And moreover he tasked me
To tell him in ryhme.
Anon at the word,
There first came one daughter
And then came another,
To second and third
The request of their brother,
And to hear how the water
Comes down at Lodore,
With its rush and its roar,
As many a time
They had seen it before.
So I told them in rhyme,
For of rhymes I had store:
And 'twas in my vocation
For their recreation
That so I should sing;
Because I was Laureate
To them and the King.

From its sources which well
In the Tarn on the fell;
From its fountains
In the mountains,
Its rills and its gills;
Through moss and through brake,
It runs and it creeps
For awhile, till it sleeps
In its own little lake.
And thence at departing,
Awakening and starting,
It runs through the reeds
And away it proceeds,

Through meadow and glade,
In sun and in shade,
And through the wood-shelter,
Among crags in its flurry,
Helter-skelter,
Hurry-scurry.
Here it comes sparkling,
And there it lies darkling;
Now smoking and frothing
Its tumult and wrath in,
Till in this rapid race
On which it is bent,
It reaches the place
Of its steep descent.

The Cataract strong
Then plunges along,
Striking and raging
As if a war waging
Its caverns and rocks among:
Rising and leaping,
Sinking and creeping,
Swelling and sweeping,
Showering and springing,
Flying and flinging,
Writhing and ringing,
Eddying and whisking,
Spouting and frisking,
Turning and twisting,
Around and around
With endless rebound!
Smiting and fighting,
A sight to delight in;
Confounding, astounding,
Dizzying and deafening the ear with its sound.
Collecting, projecting,
Receding and speeding,

And shocking and rocking,
And darting and parting,
And threading and spreading,
And whizzing and hissing,
And dripping and skipping,
And hitting and splitting,
And shining and twining,
And rattling and battling,
And shaking and quaking,
And pouring and roaring,
And waving and raving,
And tossing and crossing,
And flowing and going,
And running and stunning,

And foaming and roaming,
And dinning and spinning,
And dropping and hopping,
And working and jerking,
And guggling and struggling,
And heaving and cleaving,
And moaning and groaning;

And glittering and frittering,
And gathering and feathering,
And whitening and brightening,
And quivering and shivering,
And hurrying and scurrying,
And thundering and floundering;

Dividing and gliding and sliding,
And falling and brawling and sprawling,
And driving and riving and striving,
And sprinkling and twinkling and wrinkling,
And sounding and bounding and rounding,
And bubbling and troubling and doubling,
And grumbling and rumbling and tumbling,
And clattering and battering and shattering;
Retreating and beating and meeting and sheeting,
Delaying and straying and playing and spraying,
Advancing and prancing and glancing and dancing,
Recoiling, turmoiling and toiling and boiling,
And gleaming and streaming and steaming and beaming,
And rushing and flushing and brushing and gushing,
And flapping and rapping and clapping and slapping,
And curling and whirling and purling and twirling,
And thumping and plumping and bumping and jumping,
And dashing and flashing and splashing and clashing;
And so never ending, but always descending,
Sounds and motions for ever and ever are blending,
All at once and all o'er, with a mighty uproar,
And this way the Water comes down at Lodore.

ROBERT SOUTHEY

THE WAR SONG OF DINAS VAWR

The mountain sheep are sweeter,
But the valley sheep are fatter;
We therefore deemed it meeter
To carry off the latter.
We made an expedition;
We met a host, and quelled it;
We forced a strong position,
And killed the men who held it.

On Dyfed's richest valley,
Where herds of kine were browsing,
We made a mighty sally,
To furnish our carousing.
Fierce warriors rushed to meet us;
We met them, and o'erthrew them:
They struggled hard to beat us;
But we conquered them, and slew them.

As we drove our prize at leisure,
The king marched forth to catch us:
His rage surpassed all measure,
But his people could not match us.
He fled to his hall-pillars;
And, ere our force we led off,
Some sacked his house and cellars,
While others cut his head off.

We there, in strife bewildering,
Spilt blood enough to swim in:
We orphaned many children,
And widowed many women.
The eagles and the ravens
We glutted with our foemen;
The heroes and the cravens,
The spearmen and the bowmen.

We brought away from battle,
And much their land bemoaned them,
Two thousand head of cattle,
And the head of him who owned them:
Ednyfed, King of Dyfed,
His head was borne before us;
His wine and beasts supplied our feasts,
And his overthrow, our chorus.

THOMAS LOVE PEACOCK

ROMAN WALL BLUES

Over the heather the wet wind blows
I've lice in my tunic and a cold in my nose.

The rain comes pattering out of the sky,
I'm a Wall soldier, I don't know why.

The mist creeps over the hard grey stone,
My girl's in Tungria; I sleep alone.

Aulus goes hanging around her place,
I don't like his manners, I don't like his face.

Piso's a Christian, he worships a fish;
There'd be no kissing if he had his wish.

She gave me a ring but I diced it away;
I want my girl and I want my pay.

When I'm a veteran with only one eye
I shall do nothing but look at the sky.

W. H. AUDEN

THE WISHING-WELL

Lass, I've heard tell
That in this well
The Roman folk would chuck,
When things were going ill with them,
A coin or so for luck.

And their great Wall's a ruin on the fell,
And naught of their camp living but this well!

Ay, lass, that's so;
And yet although
Their rampart could not stand,
Who knows but luck meant getting back
Again to their own land?

So, you've chucked our last copper in the well?
Well, what luck is or isn't, who can tell!

WILFRID GIBSON

171

THE BALLAD OF AGINCOURT

Fair stood the wind for France,
When we our sails advance,
Nor now to prove our chance,
　　Longer will tarry;
But putting to the main,
At Caux, the mouth of Seine,
With all his martial train,
　　Landed King Harry.

And taking many a fort,
Furnished in warlike sort,
Marcheth towards Agincourt,
　　In happy hour;
Skirmishing day by day,
With those that stopped his way,
Where the French general lay,
　　With all his power.

Which in his height of pride,
King Henry to deride,
His ransom to provide
　　To the King sending.
Which he neglects the while,
As from a nation vile,
Yet with an angry smile,
　　Their fall portending.

And turning to his men
Quoth our brave Henry then:
'Though they to one be ten,
　　Be not amazèd.
Yet have we well begun,
Battles so bravely won,
Have ever to the sun,
　　By fame been raisèd.'

'And for myself,' quoth he,
'This me full rest shall be,
England ne'er mourn for me,
　　Nor more esteem me.

Victor I will remain,
Or on this earth lie slain,
Never shall she sustain
　　Loss to redeem me.'

'Poitiers and Cressy tell,
When most their pride did swell,
Under our swords they fell,
　　No less our skill is,
Than when our grandsire great,
Claiming the regal seat,
By many a warlike feat,
　　Lopped the French lilies.'

The Duke of York so dread
The eager vaward led;
With the main, Henry sped
　　Amongst his henchmen.
Exeter had the rear,
A braver man not there,
Oh Lord, how hot they were,
　　On the false Frenchmen!

They now to fight are gone,
Armour on armour shone,
Drum now to drum did groan,
　　To hear, was wonder;
That with cries they make,
The very earth did shake,
Trumpet to trumpet spake,
　　Thunder to thunder.

Well it thine age became,
Oh noble Erpingham,
Which didst the signal aim,
　　To our hid forces;
When from a meadow by,
Like a storm suddenly,
The English archery
　　Stuck the French horses.

With Spanish yew so strong,
Arrows a cloth-yard long,
That like to serpents stung,
　　Piercing the weather;
None from his fellow starts,
But playing manly parts,
And like true English hearts,
　　Stuck close together.

When down their bows they threw,
And forth their bilbows drew,
And on the French they flew,
　　Not one was tardy;
Arms were from shoulders sent,
Scalps to the teeth were rent,
Down the French peasants went,
　　Our men were hardy.

This while our noble King,
His broad sword brandishing,
Down the French host did ding,
　　As to o'erwhelm it;
And many a deep wound lent,
His arms with blood besprent,
And many a cruel dent
　　Bruisèd his helmet.

Gloucester, that Duke so good,
Next of the royal blood,
For famous England stood
　　With his brave brother;
Clarence, in steel so bright,
Though but a maiden knight,
Yet in that furious fight,
　　Scarce such another.

Warwick in blood did wade,
Oxford the foe invade,
And cruel slaughter made
　　Still as they ran up;
Suffolk his axe did ply,
Beaumont and Willoughby
Bare them right doughtily,
　　Ferrers and Fanhope.

Upon St Crispin's day
Fought was this noble fray,
Which fame did not delay
　　To England to carry;
Oh, when shall English men
With such acts fill a pen,
Or England breed again,
　　Such a King Harry?

MICHAEL DRAYTON

At the battle of Agincourt in 1415 the English longbowmen under Henry V scored a decisive victory against a much larger French army. Vaward: vanguard.

A SMUGGLER'S SONG

If you wake at midnight, and hear a horse's feet,
Don't go drawing back the blind, or looking in the street,
Them that asks no questions isn't told a lie.
Watch the wall, my darling, while the Gentlemen go by!
    Five and twenty ponies
    Trotting through the dark –
    Brandy for the Parson,
    'Baccy for the Clerk;
    Laces for a lady, letters for a spy,
And watch the wall, my darling, while the Gentlemen go by!

Running round the woodlump if you chance to find
Little barrels, roped and tarred, all full of brandy-wine,
Don't you shout to come and look, nor use 'em for your play.
Put the brushwood back again – and they'll be gone next day!

If you see the stable-door setting open wide;
If you see a tired horse lying down inside;
If your mother mends a coat cut about and tore;
If the lining's wet and warm – don't you ask no more!

If you meet King George's men, dressed in blue and red,
You be careful what you say, and mindful what is said.
If they call you 'pretty maid', and chuck you 'neath the chin,
Don't you tell where no one is, nor yet where no one's been!

Knocks and footsteps round the house – whistles after dark –
You've no call for running out till the house-dogs bark,
Trusty's here, and *Pincher's* here, and see how dumb they lie –
They don't fret to follow when the Gentlemen go by!

If you do as you've been told, 'likely there's a chance,
You'll be give a dainty doll, all the way from France,
With a cap of Valenciennes, and a velvet hood –
A present from the Gentlemen, along o' being good!
   Five and twenty ponies
   Trotting through the dark –
   Brandy for the Parson,
   'Baccy for the Clerk.
Them that asks no questions isn't told a lie –
Watch the wall, my darling, while the Gentlemen go by!

RUDYARD KIPLING

THE BURIAL OF SIR JOHN MOORE
AT CORUNNA

Not a drum was heard, not a funeral note,
   As his corse to the rampart we hurried;
Not a soldier discharged his farewell shot
   O'er the grave where our hero we buried.

We buried him darkly at dead of night,
   The sods with our bayonets turning;
By the struggling moonbeam's misty light,
   And the lantern dimly burning.

No useless coffin enclosed his breast,
   Not in sheet nor in shroud we wound him,
But he lay like a warrior taking his rest
   With his martial cloak around him.

Few and short were the prayers we said,
   And we spoke not a word of sorrow;
But we steadfastly gazed on the face that was dead,
   And we bitterly thought of the morrow.

We thought as we hollowed his narrow bed,
   And smoothed down his lonely pillow,
That the foe and the stranger would tread o'er his head,
   And we far away on the billow!

Lightly they'll talk of the spirit that's gone,
   And o'er his cold ashes upbraid him, –
But little he'll reck, if they let him sleep on
   In the grave where a Briton has laid him.

But half of our heavy task was done
   When the clock struck the hour for retiring;
And we heard the distant and random gun
   That the foe was sullenly firing.

Slowly and sadly we laid him down,
   From the field of his fame fresh and gory;
We carved not a line, and we raised not a stone –
   But we left him alone with his glory.

CHARLES WOLFE

Sir John Moore fell at Corunna, Northern Spain, in
1808. Reck: care.

TO HIS LOVE

He's gone, and all our plans
   Are useless indeed.
We'll walk no more on Cotswold
   Where the sheep feed
   Quietly and take no heed.

His body that was so quick
   Is not as you
Knew it, on Severn river
   Under the blue
   Driving our small boat through.

You would not know him now . . .
   But still he died
Nobly, so cover him over
   With violets of pride
   Purple from Severn side.

Cover him, cover him soon!
   And with thick-set
Masses of memoried flowers –
   Hide that red wet
   Thing I must somehow forget.

IVOR GURNEY

The composer Ivor Gurney turned poet in the trenches
of the First World War. He wrote this early
poem when his close friend F. W. Harvey was
reported missing believed dead; in fact Harvey
had been taken prisoner.

MORSE

Tuckett. Bill Tuckett. Telegraph operator, Hall's Creek
which is way out back of the Outback, but he stuck it,
quite likely liked it, despite heat, glare, dust and the lack
of diversion or doctors. Come disaster you trusted to luck,
ingenuity and pluck. This was back when nice people said pluck,
the sleevelink and green eyeshade epoch.

                Faced, though, like Bill Tuckett
with a man needing surgery right on the spot, a lot
would have done their dashes. It looked hopeless (dot dot dot)
Lift him up on the table, said Tuckett, running the key hot
till Head Office turned up a doctor who coolly instructed
up a thousand miles of wire, as Tuckett advanced slit by slit
with a safety razor blade, pioneering on into the wet,
copper-wiring the rivers off, in the first operation conducted
along dotted lines, with rum drinkers gripping the patient:
d-d-dash it, take care, Tuck!

                And the vital spark stayed unshorted.
Yallah! breathed the camelmen. Tuckett, you did it, you did it!
cried the spattered la-de-dah jodhpur-wearing Inspector of Stock.
We imagine, some weeks later, a properly laconic
convalescent averring Without you, I'd have kicked the bucket. . .
From Chungking to Burrenjuck, morse keys have mostly gone silent
and only old men meet now to chit-chat in their electric
bygone dialect. The last letter many will forget
is dit-dit-dit-dah, V for Victory. The coders' hero had speed,
resource and a touch. So ditditdit daah for Bill Tuckett.

            LES A. MURRAY

THE HIGHWAYMAN

I

The wind was a torrent of darkness among the gusty trees.
The moon was a ghostly galleon tossed upon cloudy seas.
The road was a ribbon of moonlight over the purple moor,
And the highwayman came riding –
　　Riding – riding –
The highwayman came riding, up to the old inn-door.
He'd a French cocked-hat on his forehead, a bunch of lace at his chin,
A coat of the claret velvet, and breeches of brown doe-skin;
They fitted with never a wrinkle: his boots were up to the thigh.
And he rode with a jewelled twinkle,
　　His pistol butts a-twinkle.
His rapier hilt a-twinkle, under the jewelled sky.

Over the cobbles he clattered and clashed in the dark inn-yard.
He tapped with his whip on the shutters, but all was locked and barred.
He whistled a tune to the window, and who should be waiting there
But the landlord's black-eyed daughter,
　　Bess, the landlord's daughter,
Plaiting a dark red love-knot into her long black hair.

And dark in the dark old inn-yard a stable-wicket creaked
Where Tim the ostler listened; his face was white and peaked;
His eyes were hollows of madness, his hair like mouldy hay,
But he loved the landlord's daughter,
　　The landlord's red-lipped daughter.
Dumb as a dog he listened, and he heard the robber say –

'One kiss, my bonny sweetheart, I'm after a prize tonight,
But I shall be back with the yellow gold before the morning light;
Yet, if they press me sharply, and harry me through the day,
Then look for me by moonlight,
　　Watch for me by moonlight,
I'll come to thee by moonlight, though hell should bar the way.'

He rose upright in the stirrups. He scarce could reach her hand,
But she loosened her hair in the casement. His face burnt like a brand
As the black cascade of perfume came tumbling over his breast;
And he kissed its waves in the moonlight,
    (O, sweet black waves in the moonlight!)
Then he tugged at his rein in the moonlight, and galloped away to the west.

II

He did not come in the dawning. He did not come at noon;
And out of the tawny sunset, before the rise of the moon,
When the road was a gypsy's ribbon, looping the purple moor,
A red-coat troop came marching –
    Marching – marching –
King George's men came marching, up to the old inn-door.

They said no word to the landlord. They drank his ale instead.
But they gagged his daughter, and bound her, to the foot of her narrow bed.
Two of them knelt at her casement, with muskets at their side.
There was death at every window;
    And hell at one dark window;
For Bess could see, through her casement, the road that *he* would ride.

They had tied her up to attention, with many a sniggering jest.
They had bound a musket beside her, with the muzzle beneath her breast.
'Now, keep good watch!' and they kissed her. She heard the doomed man say –
Look for me by moonlight;
   Watch for me by moonlight;
I'll come to thee by moonlight, though hell should bar the way!

She twisted her hands behind her; but all the knots held good.
She writhed her hands till her fingers were wet with sweat or blood.
They stretched and strained in the darkness, and the hours crawled by like years,
Till, now, on the stroke of midnight,
   Cold, on the stroke of midnight,
The tip of one finger touched it! The trigger at least was hers!

The tip of one finger touched it. She strove no more for the rest.
Up, she stood up to attention, with the muzzle beneath her breast.
She would not risk their hearing; she would not strive again;
For the road lay bare in the moonlight;
   Blank and bare in the moonlight;
And the blood of her veins, in the moonlight, throbbed to her love's refrain.

Tlot-tlot; tlot-tlot! Had they heard it? The horsehoofs ringing clear;
Tlot-tlot, tlot-tlot, in the distance? Were they deaf that they did not hear?
Down the ribbon of moonlight, over the brow of the hill,
The highwayman came riding –
   Riding – riding –
The red-coats looked to their priming! She stood up, straight and still.

Tlot-tlot, in the frosty silence! *Tlot-tlot,* in the echoing night!
Nearer he came and nearer. Her face was like a light.
Her eyes grew wide for a moment; she drew one last deep breath,
Then her finger moved in the moonlight,
   Her musket shattered the moonlight,
Shattered her breast in the moonlight and warned him – with her death.

He turned. He spurred to the west; he did not know who stood
Bowed, with her head o'er the musket, drenched with her own blood.
Not till the dawn he heard it, and his face grew grey to hear
How Bess, the landlord's daughter,
   The landlord's black-eyed daughter,
Had watched for her love in the moonlight, and died in the darkness there.

Back, he spurred like a madman, shouting a curse to the sky,
With the white road smoking behind him and his rapier brandished high.
Blood-red were his spurs in the golden noon; wine-red was his velvet coat;
When they shot him down on the highway,
   Down like a dog on the highway,
And he lay in his blood on the highway, with a bunch of lace at his throat.

And still of a winter's night, they say, when the wind is in the trees,
When the moon is a ghostly galleon tossed upon cloudy seas,
When the road is a ribbon of moonlight over the purple moor,
A highwayman comes riding —
   Riding — riding —
A highwayman comes riding, up to the old inn-door.

Over the cobbles he clatters and clangs in the dark inn-yard.
He taps with his whip on the shutters, but all is locked and barred.
He whistles a tune to the window, and who should be waiting there
But the landlord's black-eyed daughter,
   Bess, the landlord's daughter,
Plaiting a dark red love-knot into her long black hair.

ALFRED NOYES

THE LISTENERS

'Is there anybody there?' said the Traveller,
  Knocking on the moonlit door;
And his horse in the silence champed the grasses
  Of the forest's ferny floor:
And a bird flew up out of the turret,
  Above the Traveller's head:
And he smote upon the door again a second time;
  'Is there anybody there?' he said.
But no one descended to the Traveller;
  No head from the leaf-fringed sill
Leaned over and looked into his grey eyes,
  Where he stood perplexed and still.
But only a host of phantom listeners
  That dwelt in the lone house then
Stood listening in the quiet of the moonlight
  To that voice from the world of men:
Stood thronging the faint moonbeams on the dark stair,
  That goes down to the empty hall,
Hearkening in an air stirred and shaken
  By the lonely Traveller's call.
And he felt in his heart their strangeness,
  Their stillness answering his cry,
While his horse moved, cropping the dark turf,
  'Neath the starred and leafy sky;
For he suddenly smote on the door, even
  Louder, and lifted his head: –
'Tell them I came, and no one answered,
  That I kept my word,' he said.
Never the least stir made the listeners,
  Though every word he spake
Fell echoing through the shadowiness of the still house
From the one man left awake:
Ay, they heard his foot upon the stirrup,
  And the sound of iron on stone,
And how the silence surged softly backward,
  When the plunging hoofs were gone.

WALTER DE LA MARE

THE WAY THROUGH THE WOODS

They shut the road through the woods
Seventy years ago.
Weather and rain have undone it again,
And now you would never know
There was once a road through the woods

Before they planted the trees.
It is underneath the coppice and heath
And the thin anemones.
Only the keeper sees
That, where the ring-dove broods,
And the badgers roll at ease,
There was once a road through the woods.

Yet, if you enter the woods
Of a summer evening late,
When the night-air cools on the trout-ringed pools
Where the otter whistles his mate,
(They fear not men in the woods,
Because they see so few.)
You will hear the beat of a horse's feet,
And the swish of a skirt in the dew,
Steadily cantering through
The misty solitudes,
As though they perfectly knew
The old lost road through the woods . . .
But there is no road through the woods.

RUDYARD KIPLING

THE MAGPIES

When Tom and Elizabeth took the farm
The bracken made their bed,
And *Quardle oodle ardle wardle doodle*
The magpies said.

Tom's hand was strong to the plough
Elizabeth's lips were red,
And *Quardle oodle ardle wardle doodle*
The magpies said.

Year in year out they worked
While the pines grew overhead,
And *Quardle oodle ardle wardle doodle*
The magpies said.

But all the beautiful crops soon went
To the mortgage-man instead,
And *Quardle oodle ardle wardle doodle*
The magpies said.

Elizabeth is dead now (it's years ago);
Old Tom went light in the head;
And *Quardle oodle ardle wardle doodle*
The magpies said.

The farm's still there. Mortgage corporations
Couldn't give it away.
And *Quardle oodle ardle wardle doodle*
The magpies say.

DENIS GLOVER

THE OUTLAW OF LOCH LENE

O many a day have I made good ale in the glen,
That came not of stream or malt, like the brewing of men:
My bed was the ground; my roof, the green-wood above;
And the wealth that I sought, one far kind glance from my Love.

Alas, on the night when the horses I drove from the field
That I was not near from terror my angel to shield!
She stretched forth her arms; her mantle she flung to the wind,
And swam o'er Loch Lene, her outlawed lover to find.

O would that a freezing sleet-winged tempest did sweep,
And I and my love were alone, far off on the deep;
I'd ask not a ship, or a bark, or a pinnace, to save –
With her hand round my waist, I'd fear not the wind or the wave.

'Tis down by the lake where the wild tree fringes its sides,
The maid of my heart, my fair one of Heaven resides:
I think, as at eve she wanders its mazes among,
The birds go to sleep by the sweet wild twist of her song.

JEREMIAH JOHN CALLANAN

LA BELLE DAME SANS MERCI

O what can ail thee Knight at arms,
　　Alone and palely loitering?
The sedge has withered from the Lake,
　　And no birds sing!

O what can ail thee Knight at arms,
　　So haggard, and so woe begone?
The Squirrel's granary is full
　　And the harvest's done.

I see a lilly on thy brow
　　With anguish moist and fever dew,
And on thy cheeks a fading rose
　　Fast withereth too.

I met a Lady in the meads
　　Full beautiful, a faery's child,
Her hair was long, her foot was light,
　　And her eyes were wild.

I made a Garland for her head,
　　And bracelets too, and fragrant Zone;
She look'd at me as she did love
　　And made sweet moan.

I set her on my pacing steed
　　And nothing else saw all day long;
For sidelong would she bend and sing
　　A faery's song.

She found me roots of relish sweet
　　And honey wild and manna dew;
And sure in language strange she said –
　　I love thee true.

She took me to her elfin grot,
　　And there she wept and sigh'd full sore;
And there I shut her wild wild eyes
　　With kisses four.

And there she lulled me asleep,
　　And there I dream'd, Ah Woe betide!
The latest dream I ever dreamt
　　On the cold hill side.

I saw pale Kings, and Princes too,
　　Pale warriors, death pale were they all;
They cried, 'La Belle Dame sans Merci
　　Thee hath in thrall!'

I saw their starv'd lips in the gloam
　　With horrid warning gaped wide,
And I awoke, and found me here
　　On the cold hill's side.

And this is why I sojourn here
　　Alone and palely loitering,
Though the sedge is withered from the Lake,
　　And no birds sing.

JOHN KEATS

'HER STRONG ENCHANTMENTS FAILING'

Her strong enchantments failing,
  Her towers of fear in wreck,
Her limbecks dried of poisons
  And the knife at her neck,

The Queen of air and darkness
  Begins to shrill and cry,
'O young man, O my slayer,
  Tomorrow you shall die.'

O Queen of air and darkness,
  I think 'tis truth you say,
And I shall die tomorrow;
  But you will die today.

A. E. HOUSMAN

RICHARD CORY

Whenever Richard Cory went down town,
We people on the pavement looked at him:
He was a gentleman from sole to crown,
Clean favored, and imperially slim.

he was always quietly arrayed,
And he was always human when he talked;
But still he fluttered pulses when he said,
'Good-morning,' and he glittered when he walked.

And he was rich — yes, richer than a king —
And admirably schooled in every grace:
In fine, we thought that he was everything
To make us wish that we were in his place.

So on we worked, and waited for the light,
And went without the meat, and cursed the bread;
And Richard Cory, one calm summer night,
Went home and put a bullet through his head.

EDWIN ARLINGTON ROBINSON

LORD RANDAL

'O where hae ye been, Lord Randal, my son?
O where hae ye been, my handsome young man?'
'I hae been to the wild wood; mother, make my bed soon,
For I'm weary wi' hunting, and fain wald lie down.'

'Where gat ye your dinner, Lord Randal, my son?
Where gat ye your dinner, my handsome young man?'
'I dined wi' my true-love; mother, make my bed soon,
For I'm weary wi' hunting, and fain wald lie down.'

'What gat ye to your dinner, Lord Randal, my son?
What gat ye to your dinner, my handsome young man?'
'I gat eels boiled in broo'; mother, make my bed soon,
For I'm weary wi' hunting, and fain wald lie down.'

'What became of your bloodhounds, Lord Randal, my son?
What became of your bloodhounds, my handsome young man?'
'O they swelled and they died; mother, make my bed soon,
For I'm weary wi' hunting, and fain wald lie down.'

'O I fear ye are poisoned, Lord Randal, my son!
O I fear ye are poisoned, my handsome young man!'
'O yes! I am poisoned; mother, make my bed soon,
For I'm sick at the heart, and I fain wald lie down.'

TRADITIONAL

broo: broth

FRANKIE AND JOHNNY

Frankie and Johnny were lovers,
Lordy, how they could love,
Swore to be true to each other,
True as the stars above,
    He was her man, but he done her wrong.

Little Frankie was a good gal,
As everybody knows,
She did all the work around the house,
And pressed her Johnny's clothes,
    He was her man, but he done her wrong.

Johnny was a yeller man,
With coal black, curly hair,
Everyone up in St Louis
Thought he was a millionaire,
    He was her man, but he done her wrong.

Frankie went down to the bar-room,
Called for a bottle of beer,
Says, 'Looky here, Mister Bartender,
Has my lovin' Johnny been here?
    He is my man, and he's doin' me wrong.'

'I will not tell you no story,
I will not tell you no lie.
Johnny left here about an hour ago,
With a gal named Nelly Bly,
    He is your man and he's doing you wrong.'

Little Frankie went down Broadway,
With her pistol in her hand,
Said, 'Stand aside you chorus gals,
I'm lookin' for my man,
    He is my man, and he's doin' me wrong.'

The first time she shot him, he staggered,
The next time she shot him, he fell,
The last time she shot, O Lawdy,
There was a new man's face in hell,
    She shot her man, for doin' her wrong.

'Turn me over doctor,
Turn me over slow,
I got a bullet in my left hand side,
Great God, it's hurtin' me so.
    I was her man, but I done her wrong.'

It was a rubber-tyred buggy,
Decorated hack,
Took poor Johnny to the graveyard,
Brought little Frankie back,
    He was her man, but he done her wrong.

It was not murder in the first degree,
It was not murder in the third,
A woman simply dropped her man
Like a hunter drops his bird,
    She shot her man, for doin' her wrong.

The last time I saw Frankie,
She was sittin' in the 'lectric chair,
Waitin' to go and meet her God
With the sweat runnin' out of her hair.
    She shot her man, for doin' her wrong.

Walked on down Broadway
As far as I could see,
All I could hear was a two string bow
Playin' *'Nearer my God to thee'*,
    He was her man, and he done her wrong.

TRADITIONAL

189

THE DOUGLAS TRAGEDY

'Rise up, rise up, now, Lord Douglas,' she says,
    'And put on your armour so bright;
Let it never be said that a daughter of thine
    Was married to a lord under night.

'Rise up, rise up, my seven bold sons,
    And put on your armour so bright,
And take better care of your youngest sister,
    For your eldest's awa the last night.'

He's mounted her on a milk-white steed,
    And himself on a dapple grey,
With a bugelet horn hung down by his side,
    And lightly they rode away.

Lord William lookit o'er his left shoulder,
    To see what he could see,
And there he spy'd her seven brethren bold,
    Come riding over the lee.

'Light down, light down, Lady Marg'ret,' he said,
    'And hold my steed in your hand,
Until that against your seven brethren bold,
    And your father, I mak a stand.'

She held his steed in her milk-white hand,
    And never shed one tear,
Until that she saw her seven brethren fa',
    And her father hard fighting, who loved her so dear

'O hold your hand, Lord William!' she said,
    'For your strokes they are wond'rous sair;
True lovers I can get many a ane,
    But a father I can never get mair.'

O she's ta'en out her handkerchief,
    It was o' the holland sae fine,
And aye she dighted her father's bloody wounds,
    That were redder than the wine.

'O chuse, O chuse, Lady Marg'ret,' he said,
    'O whether will ye gang or bide?'
'I'll gang, I'll gang, Lord William,' she said,
    'For ye have left me no other guide.'

He's lifted her on a milk-white steed,
    And himself on a dapple grey,
With a bugelet horn hung down by his side,
    And slowly they baith rade away.

O they rade on, and on they rade,
　And a' by the light of the moon,
Until they came to yon wan water,
　And there they lighted down.

They lighted down to tak a drink
　Of the spring that ran sae clear;
And down the stream ran his gude heart's blood
　And sair she gan to fear.

'Hold up, hold up, Lord William,' she says,
　'For I fear that you are slain!'
'''Tis naething but the shadow of my scarlet cloak,
　That shines in the water sae plain.'

O they rade on, and on they rade,
　And a' by the light of the moon,
Until they cam to his mother's ha' door,
　And there they lighted down.

'Get up, get up, lady mother,' he says,
　'Get up, and let me in! –
Get up, get up, lady mother, he says,
　'For this night my fair lady I've win.

'O mak my bed, lady mother,' he says,
　'O mak it braid and deep!
And lay Lady Marg'ret close at my back,
　And the sounder I will sleep.'

Lord William was dead lang ere midnight,
　Lady Marg'ret lang ere day –
And all true lovers that go thegither,
　May they have mair luck than they!

Lord William was buried in St Marie's kirk,
　Lady Margaret in Marie's quire;
Out o' the lady's grave grew a bonny red rose,
　And out o' the knight's a brier.

And they twa met, and they twa plat,
　And fain they wad be near;
And a' the warld might ken right weel,
　They were twa lovers dear.

But bye and rade the Black Douglas,
　And wow but he was rough!
For he pulled up the bonny brier,
　And flang'd in St Mary's Loch.

TRADITIONAL

dighted: wiped
plat: intertwined

YOUNG LOCHINVAR

O, young Lochinvar is come out of the west,
Through all the wide Border his steed was the best;
And save his good broadsword he weapons had none,
He rode all unarmed, and he rode all alone.
So faithful in love, and so dauntless in war,
There never was knight like the young Lochinvar.

He stayed not for brake, and he stopped not for stone,
He swam the Esk river where ford there was none;
But ere he alighted at Netherby gate,
The bride had consented, the gallant came late:
For a laggard in love, and a dastard in war,
Was to wed the fair Ellen of brave Lochinvar.

So boldly he entered the Netherby Hall,
Among bridesmen, and kinsmen, and brothers, and all:
Then spoke the bride's father, his hand on his sword
(For the poor craven bridegroom said never a word),
'O come ye in peace here, or come ye in war,
Or to dance at our bridal, young Lord Lochinvar?'

'I long wooed your daughter, my suit you denied –
Love swells like the Solway, but ebbs like its tide –
And now am I come, with this lost love of mine,
To lead but one measure, drink one cup of wine.
There are maidens in Scotland more lovely by far,
That would gladly be bride to the young Lochinvar.'

The bride kissed the goblet: the knight took it up,
He quaffed off the wine, and he threw down the cup.
She looked down to blush, and she looked up to sigh,
With a smile on her lips, and a tear in her eye.
He took her soft hand, ere her mother could bar –
'Now tread we a measure!' said young Lochinvar.

So stately his form, and so lovely her face,
That never a hall such a galliard did grace;
While her mother did fret, and her father did fume,
And the bridegroom stood dangling his bonnet and plume;
And the bride-maidens whispered, ''Twere better by far,
To have matched our fair cousin with young Lochinvar.'

One touch to her hand, and one word in her ear,
When they reached the hall door, and the charger stood near;
So light to the croupe the fair lady he swung,
So light to the saddle before her he sprung!
'She is won! we are gone, over bank, bush, and scaur;
They'll have fleet steeds that follow,' quoth young Lochinvar.

There was mounting 'mong Graemes of the Netherby clan;
Forsters, Fenwicks, and Musgraves, they rode and they ran:
There was racing and chasing on Cannobie Lee,
But the lost bride of Netherby ne'er did they see.
So daring in love, and so dauntless in war,
Have ye e'er heard of gallant like young Lochinvar?

SIR WALTER SCOTT

OUR SHIP SHE LIES IN HARBOUR

There lays a ship in the harbour
Just ready to set sail,
Crying, Heaven shall be my guard, my love,
Till I return again.

Says the old man to the daughter,
What makes you so lament?
Oh the lad that you have sent to sea,
He can give my heart content.

So if that's your inclination,
The old man did reply,
I hope he will continue there
And on the seas may die.

So when nine long weeks was over
And ten long tedious days
I saw the ship come shivering in
With my true love home from sea.

Yonder sits my angel,
She's waiting there for me
And tomorrow to the church we'll go
And married we will be.

So when we got into the church
And turning back again
I met my own rude father
And several gentlemen.

So he says, My dearest daughter,
Five hundred I will give
If you forsake that sailor lad
And go with me to live.

No, it's not your gold that glitters
Nor yet your silver that shines,
I'm married to the lad I love
And I'm happy in my mind.

TRADITIONAL

THE FORSAKEN MERMAN

Come, dear children, let us away;
Down and away below!
Now my brothers call from the bay,
Now the great winds shoreward blow,
Now the salt tides seaward flow;
Now the wild white horses play,
Champ and chafe and toss in the spray.
Children dear, let us away!
This way, this way!

Call her once before you go –
Call once yet!
In a voice that she will know:
'Margaret! Margaret!'
Children's voices should be dear
(Call once more) to a mother's ear;
Children's voices, wild with pain –
Surely she will come again!
Call her once and come away;
This way, this way!
'Mother dear, we cannot stay!
The wild white horses foam and fret.'
Margaret! Margaret!

Come, dear children, come away down;
Call no more!
One last look at the white-wall'd town,
And the little grey church on the windy shore,
Then come down!
She will not come though you call all day;
Come away, come away!

Children dear, was it yesterday
We heard the sweet bells over the bay?
In the caverns where we lay,
Through the surf and through the swell,
The far-off sound of a silver bell?

Sand-strewn caverns, cool and deep,
Where the winds are all asleep;
Where the spent lights quiver and gleam,
Where the salt weed sways in the stream,
Where the sea-beasts, ranged all round,
Feed in the ooze of their pasture-ground;
Where the sea-snakes coil and twine,
Dry their mail and bask in the brine;
Where great whales come sailing by,
Sail and sail, with unshut eye,
Round the world for ever and aye?
When did music come this way?
Children dear, was it yesterday?

Children dear, was it yesterday
(Call yet once) that she went away?
Once she sate with you and me,
On a red gold throne in the heart of the sea,
And the youngest sate on her knee.
She comb'd its bright hair, and she tended it well,
When down swung the sound of a far-off bell.
She sigh'd, she look'd up through the clear green sea;
She said: 'I must go, for my kinsfolk pray
In the little grey church on the shore today.
'Twill be Easter-time in the world – ah me!
And I lose my pool soul, Merman! here with thee.'
I said: 'Go up, dear heart, through the waves;
Say thy prayer, and come back to the kind sea-caves!'
She smiled, she went up through the surf in the bay.
Children dear, was it yesterday?

　Children dear, were we long alone?
'The sea grows stormy, the little ones moan;
Long prayers,' I said, 'in the world they say;
Come!' I said; and we rose through the surf in the bay.
We went up the beach, by the sandy down
Where the sea-stocks bloom, to the white-wall'd town;
Through the narrow paved streets, where all was still,
To the little grey church on the windy hill.

From the church came a murmur of folk at their prayers,
But we stood without in the cold blowing airs.
We climb'd on the graves, on the stones worn with rains,
And we gazed up the aisle through the small leaded panes.
She sate by the pillar; we saw her clear:
'Margaret, hist! come quick, we are here!
Dear heart,' I said, 'we are long alone;
The sea grows stormy, the little ones moan.'
But, ah, she gave me never a look,
For her eyes were seal'd to the holy book!
Loud prays the priest; shut stands the door.
Come away, children, call no more!
Come away, come down, call no more!

    Down, down, down!
Down to the depths of the sea!
She sits at her wheel in the humming town,
Singing most joyfully.
Hark what she sings: 'O joy, O joy,
For the humming street, and the child with its toy!
For the priest, and the bell, and the holy well;
For the wheel where I spun,
And the blessed light of the sun!'

And so she sings her fill,
Singing most joyfully,
'Till the spindle drops from her hand,
And the whizzing wheel stands still.
She steals to the window, and looks at the sand,
And over the sand at the sea;
And her eyes are set in a stare;
And anon there breaks a sigh,
And anon there drops a tear,
From a sorrow-clouded eye,
And a heart sorrow-laden,
A long, long sigh;
For the cold strange eyes of a little Mermaiden
And the gleam of her golden hair.

 Come away, away children;
Come children, come down!
The hoarse wind blows coldly;
Lights shine in the town.
She will start from her slumber
When gusts shake the door;
She will hear the winds howling,
Will hear the waves roar.
We shall see, while above us
The waves roar and whirl,
A ceiling of amber,
A pavement of pearl.
Singing: 'Here came a mortal,
But faithless was she!
And alone dwell for ever
The kings of the sea.'

But, children, at midnight,
When soft the winds blow,
When clear falls the moonlight,
When spring-tides are low;
When sweet airs come seaward
From heaths starr'd with broom,
And high rocks throw mildly
On the blanch'd sands a gloom;

Up the still, glistening beaches,
Up the creeks we will hie,
Over banks of bright seaweed
The ebb-tide leaves dry.

We will gaze, from the sand-hills,
At the white, sleeping town;
At the church on the hill-side –
And then come back down.
Singing: 'There dwells a loved one,
But cruel is she!
She left lonely for ever
The kings of the sea.'

MATTHEW ARNOLD

SONG OF THE GALLEY-SLAVES

We pulled for you when the wind was against us and
   the sails were low.
     Will you never let us go?
We ate bread and onions when you took towns, or ran aboard
   quickly when you were beaten back by the foe.
The Captains walked up and down the deck in fair weather
   singing songs, but we were below,
We fainted with our chins on the oars and you did not see
   that we were idle, for we still swung to and fro.
     Will you never let us go?
The salt made the oar-handles like shark-skin; our knees
   were cut to the bone with salt-cracks; our hair was stuck
   to our foreheads; and our lips were cut to the gums, and
   you whipped us because we could not row.
     Will you never let us go?
But, in a little time, we shall run out of the port-holes as the
   water runs along the oar-blade, and though you tell the
   others to row after us you will never catch us till you
   catch the oar-thresh and tie up the winds in the belly
   of the sail. Aho!
     Will you never let us go?

RUDYARD KIPLING

THE LAND OF

WHIPPERGINNY

THE LAND OF WHIPPERGINNY

Come closer yet, my honeysuckle, my sweetheart Jinny:
    A low sun is gilding the bloom of the wood –
Is it Heaven, or Hell, or the Land of Whipperginny
    That holds this fairy lustre, not yet understood?

For stern proud psalms from the chapel on the moors
    Waver in the night wind, their firm rhythm broken,
Lugubriously twisted to a howling of whores
    Or lent an airy glory too strange to be spoken.

Soon the risen Moon will peer down with pity,
    Drawing us in secret by an ivory gate
To the fruit-plats and fountains of her silver city
    Where lovers need not argue the tokens of fate.

ROBERT GRAVES

BOOMERANG

Behold! wood into bird and bird to wood again.
A brown-winged bird from the hand of a brown man.

Elbow of wood from flexed elbow of bone
to a swift hawk has amazingly grown

that mounts the sky, sun in its wings,
up, up, over the far tree fluttering

where it turns as if seized with doubt in the air.
Looks back down to the man carved there

and, afraid of the gift of sudden blood,
beats back to his hand and melts once more to wood.

WILLIAM HART-SMITH

INVOCATION

Dolphin plunge, fountain play.
Fetch me far and far away.

Fetch me far my nursery toys,
Fetch me far my mother's hand,
Fetch me far the painted joys.

And when the painted cock shall crow
Fetch me far my waking day
That I may dance before I go.

Fetch me far the breeze in the heat,
Fetch me far the curl of the wave,
Fetch me far the face in the street.

And when the other faces throng
Fetch me far a place in the mind
Where only truthful things belong.

Fetch me far a moon in a tree,
Fetch me far a phrase of the wind,
Fetch me far the verb To Be.

And when the last horn burns the hills
Fetch me far one draught of grace
To quench my thirst before it kills.

Dolphin plunge, fountain play.
Fetch me far and far away.

LOUIS MACNEICE

'SHAKE OFF YOUR HEAVY TRANCE'

Shake off your heavy trance,
    And leap into a dance
Such as no mortals use to tread;
    Fit only for Apollo
To play to, for the moon to lead,
    And all the stars to follow!

SIR FRANCIS BEAUMONT

JOHN CONNU RIDER

When John Connu come', he come' wit' style
An' wit' plenty noise an' plenty practice
From way back 'cross plantation lawn
An' 'ill-an'-gully rider.

John Connu got 'orse-'ead an' 'ouse-top
An' king-'ead an' bird-body
An' 'nough other t'ings that frighten
Mos' o' we, bad.

John Connu sing' an' John Connu dance'
An' Connu walk' 'ard
An' Connu walk' sof'
An' Connu' eye got eyewater in it
When he laugh'.

ANDREW SALKEY

John Connu (John the Unknown) is a carnival
character in Jamaica.

THE SONG OF WANDERING AENGUS

I went out to the hazel wood,
Because a fire was in my head,
And cut and peeled a hazel wand,
And hooked a berry to a thread;
And when white moths were on the wing,
And moth-like stars were flickering out,
I dropped the berry in a stream
And caught a little silver trout.

When I had laid it on the floor
I went to blow the fire aflame,
But something rustled on the floor,
And some one called me by my name:

It had become a glimmering girl
With apple blossom in her hair
Who called me by my name and ran
And faded through the brightening air.

Though I am old with wandering
Through hollow lands and hilly lands,
I will find out where she has gone,
And kiss her lips and take her hands;
And walk among long dappled grass,
And pluck till time and times are done
The silver apples of the moon,
The golden apples of the sun.

W. B. YEATS

I SAW A PEACOCK

I saw a Peacock with a fiery tail,
I saw a blazing Comet drop down hail,
I saw a Cloud with ivy circled round,
I saw a sturdy Oak creep on the ground,
I saw a Pismire swallow up a whale,
I saw a raging Sea brim full of ale,
I saw a Venice Glass sixteen foot deep,
I saw a Well full of men's tears that weep,
I saw their Eyes all in a flame of fire,
I saw a House as big as the moon and higher,
I saw the Sun even in the midst of night,
I saw the Man that saw this wondrous sight.

TRADITIONAL

Pismire: ant

'HOW MANY MILES TO BABYLON?'

How many miles to Babylon?
Threescore and ten, Sir.

Can I get there by candlelight?
Oh yes, and back again, Sir.

If your heels are nimble and light,
You may get there by candlelight.

TRADITIONAL

ROMANCE

When I was but thirteen or so
   I went into a golden land;
Chimborazo, Cotopaxi
   Took me by the hand.

My father died, my brother too,
   They passed like fleeting dreams.
I stood where Popocatapetl
   In the sunlight gleams.

I dimly heard the master's voice
   And boys far off at play.
Chimborazo, Cotopaxi
   Had stolen me away.

I walked in a great golden dream
   To and fro from school –
Shining Popocatapetl
   The dusty streets did rule.

I walked home with a gold dark boy,
   And never a word I'd say,
Chimborazo, Cotopaxi
   Had taken my speech away:

I gazed entranced upon his face
   Fairer than any flower –
O shining Popocatapetl,
   It was thy magic hour:

The houses, people, traffic seemed
   Thin fading dreams by day,
Chimborazo, Cotopaxi
   They had stolen my soul away.

W. J. TURNER

ELDORADO

Gaily bedight,
   A gallant knight,
In sunshine and in shadow,
   Had journeyed long,
   Singing a song,
In search of Eldorado.

But he grew old –
   This knight so bold –
And o'er his heart a shadow
   Fell as he found
   No spot of ground
That looked like Eldorado.

And, as his strength
   Failed him at length,
He met a pilgrim shadow:
   'Shadow,' said he,
   'Where can it be,
This land of Eldorado?'

'Over the mountains
   Of the Moon,
Down the valley of the Shadow,
   Ride, boldly ride,'
   The shade replied,
'If you seek for Eldorado.'

EDGAR ALLAN POE

LOVING MAD TOM

From the hag and hungry goblin
That into rags would rend ye
All the spirits that stand by the naked man
In the Book of Moons defend ye!
That of your five sound senses
You never be forsaken
Nor wander from yourselves with Tom
Abroad to beg your bacon.

    While I do sing 'Any food, any feeding,
    Feeding, drink, or clothing'
    Come dame or maid, be not afraid,
    Poor Tom will injure nothing.

O thirty bare years have I
Twice twenty been enragèd,
And of forty been three times fifteen
In durance soundly cagèd
On the lordly lofts of Bedlam,
With stubble soft and dainty,
Brave bracelets strong, sweet whip's ding dong,
With wholesome hunger plenty.

    And now I sing etc.

With a thought I took for Maudlin
And a cruise of cockle pottage
With a thing thus tall, sky bless you all,
I befell into this dotage.
I slept not since the Conquest,
Till then I never wakèd,
Till the roguish boy of love where I lay
Me found and stripped me naked.

    And now I sing etc.

When I short have shorn my sour face
And swigged my horny barrel
In an oaken inn I pound my skin
As a suit of gilt apparel.

The moon's my constant Mistress
And the lonely owl my marrow,
The flaming drake and the nightcrow make
Me music to my sorrow.

    And now I sing etc.

The palsy plagues my pulses
When I prig their pigs or pullen,
Your culvers take, or matchless make
Your chanticleer, or sullen;
When I want provant, with Humphrey
I sup; and when benighted
I repose in Paul's with waking souls,
Yet never am affrighted.

    But I do sing etc.

I know more than Apollo,
For oft when he lies sleeping
I see the stars at bloody wars
In the wounded welkin weeping;
The moon embrace her shepherd
And the queen of Love her warrior,
While the first doth horn the star of morn
And the next the heavenly Farrier.

    While I do sing etc.

The Gipsy snap and Pedro
Are none of Tom's comradoes.
The punk I scorn and the cutpurse sworn
And the roaring boys' bravado.
The meek, the white, the gentle,
Me handle, touch, and spare not,
But those that cross Tom Rynosseros
Do what the panther dare not.

    Although I sing etc.

With an host of furious fancies,
Whereof I am commander,
With a burning spear, and a horse of air,
To the wilderness I wander.
By a knight of ghosts and shadows
I summoned am to tourney,
Ten leagues beyond the wide world's end.

Me thinks it is no journey.

Yet will I sing 'Any food, any feeding,
Feeding, drink or clothing'
Come dame or maid, be not afraid,
Poor Tom will injure nothing.

ANONYMOUS

BUNCHES OF GRAPES

'Bunches of grapes,' says Timothy;
'Pomegranates pink,' says Elaine;
'A junket of cream and a cranberry tart
    For me,' says Jane.

'Love-in-a-mist,' says Timothy;
'Primroses pale,' says Elaine;
'A nosegay of pinks and mignonette
    For me,' says Jane.

'Chariots of gold,' says Timothy;
'Silvery wings,' says Elaine;
'A bumpity ride in a wagon of hay
    For me,' says Jane.

WALTER DE LA MARE

'THREE PLUM BUNS'

Three plum buns
   To eat here at the stile
In the clover meadow,
   For we have walked a mile.

One for you, and one for me,
   And one left over:
Give it to the boy who shouts
   To scare sheep from the clover.

CHRISTINA ROSSETTI

DAWLISH FAIR

Over the Hill and over the Dale,
   And over the Bourne to Dawlish,
Where ginger-bread wives have a scanty sale,
   And ginger-bread nuts are smallish.

JOHN KEATS

KING ARTHUR

When Good King Arthur ruled the land,
He was a goodly king;
He stole three pecks of barley-meal,
To make a bag-pudding.

A bag-pudding the Queen did make,
And stuffed it full of plums,
And in it put great lumps of fat,
As big as my two thumbs.

The King and Queen sat down to dine,
And all the court beside;
And what they could not eat that night,
The Queen next morning fried.

TRADITIONAL

'AMID THE DERRINGERS I RIDE'

Amid the derringers I ride,
My graphic hat eskew:
Toupees tumble in the tide,
And the shy napkin, kapok-eyed,
Dottles the dervish dew.

The numismatic moon above
Makes sleezy all the sky;
The farad sizzles to his love;
The dermatitis and the dove
Go scapulary by.

And where the logarithm blows
Under the benzine tree,
Creatures all natty and nodose,
And balusters with buckish toes,
Run friable and free.

Oh the great mountain's gravid peak,
Tipped with the wind-blown crith,
Makes creeping carotids seem weak,
That through the high saliva sneak
And pipe their piteous pith.

When dawn breaks hispid on that hill
And all the schedules shine,
The bouillabaisse will ope its bill,
And I will mount my trusty twill
And cross from crine to crine.

Till, where the piccalilli spring,
I find a millibar:
And there my figment down I'll fling,
And tune my parasite, and sing
A sonorous raffia.

EDWARD BLISHEN

*'When I use a word,' says Humpty Dumpty, 'it means just what
I choose it to mean — neither more nor less.' Edward Blishen's
poem stems from a party game in which Humpty's rule applies.*

THE YULE DAYS

The king sent his lady on the first Yule day,
A papingo-aye;
Wha learns my carol and carries it away?

The king sent his lady on the second Yule day,
Three partridges, a papingo-aye;
Wha learns my carol and carries it away?

The king sent his lady on the third Yule day,
Three plovers, three partridges, a papingo-aye;
Wha learns my carol and carries it away?

The king sent his lady on the fourth Yule day,
A goose that was gray,
Three plovers, three partridges, a papingo-aye;
Wha learns my carol and carries it away?

The king sent his lady on the fifth Yule day,
Three starlings, a goose that was gray,
Three plovers, three partridges, and a papingo-aye;
Wha learns my carol and carries it away?

The king sent his lady on the sixth Yule day,
Three goldspinks, three starlings, a goose that was gray,
Three plovers, three partridges, and a papingo-aye;
Wha learns my carol and carries it away?

The king sent his lady on the seventh Yule day,
A bull that was brown, three goldspinks, three starlings,
A goose that was gray,
Three plovers, three partridges, and a papingo-aye;
Wha learns my carol and carries it away?

The king sent his lady on the eighth Yule day,
Three ducks a-merry laying, a bull that was brown —

[*The rest to follow as before*]

The king sent his lady on the ninth Yule day,
Three swans a-merry swimming –   [*As before*]

The king sent his lady on the tenth Yule day,
An Arabian baboon –   [*As before*]

The king sent his lady on the eleventh Yule day,
Three hinds a-merry hunting –   [*As before*]

The king sent his lady on the twelfth Yule day,
Three maids a-merry dancing –   [*As before*]

The king sent his lady on the thirteenth Yule day,
Three stalks o' merry corn, three maids a-merry dancing,
Three hinds a-merry hunting, an Arabian baboon,
Three swans a-merry swimming,
Three ducks a-merry laying, a bull that was brown,
Three goldspinks, three starlings, a goose that was gray,
Three plovers, three partridges, a papingo-aye;
Wha learns my carol and carries it away?

TRADITIONAL

Yule: Christmas
papingo-aye; peacock
goldspink: goldfinch

LEGEND

The blacksmith's boy went out with a rifle
and a black dog running behind.
Cobwebs snatched at his feet,
rivers hindered him,
thorn-branches caught at his eyes to make him blind
and the sky turned into an unlucky opal,
but he didn't mind,
I can break branches, I can swim rivers, I can stare out any spider I meet,
said he to his dog and his rifle.

The blacksmith's boy went over the paddocks
with his old black hat on his head.
Mountains jumped in his way,
rocks rolled down on him,
and the old crow cried, 'You'll soon be dead.'
And the rain came down like mattocks.
But he only said
I can climb mountains, I can dodge rocks, I can shoot an old crow any day,
and he went on over the paddocks.

When he came to the end of the day the sun began falling.
Up came the night ready to swallow him,
like the barrel of a gun,
like an old black hat,
like a black dog hungry to follow him.
Then the pigeon, the magpie and the dove began wailing
and the grass lay down to pillow him.
His rifle broke, his hat blew away and his dog was gone
and the sun was falling.

But in front of the night the rainbow stood on the mountain,
just as his heart foretold.
He ran like a hare,
he climbed like a fox;
he caught it in his hands, the colours and the cold –
like a bar of ice, like the column of a fountain,
like a ring of gold.
The pigeon, the magpie and the dove flew up to stare,
and the grass stood up again on the mountain.

The blacksmith's boy hung the rainbow on his shoulder
instead of his broken gun.
Lizards ran out to see,
snakes made way for him,
and the rainbow shone as brightly as the sun.
All the world said, Nobody is braver, nobody is bolder,
nobody else has done
anything to equal it. He went home as bold as he could be
with the swinging rainbow on his shoulder.

JUDITH WRIGHT

THE DERBY RAM

As I was going to Derby,
   'Twas on a market day,
I saw the finest ram, sir,
   That ever was fed on hay.
This ram was fat behind, sir,
   This ram was fat before,
This ram was ten yards high, sir,
   If he wasn't a little more.
     That's a lie, that's a lie,
     That's a tid i fa la lie.

Now the wool upon his belly, sir,
   Went draggling on the ground,
And that was took to Derby, sir,
   And sold for ten thousand pound.
Now the wool upon his tail, sir,
   Was ten inches and an ell,
And that was took to Derby, sir,
   To toll the old market-bell.
     That's a lie, that's a lie,
     That's a tid i fa la lie.

Now the man that fed this ram, sir,
   He fed him twice a day,
And each time that he fed him, sir,
   He ate a rick of hay.
Now the man that watered this ram, sir,
   He watered him twice a day,
And each time that he watered him
   He drank the river dry.
     That's a lie, that's a lie,
     That's a tid i fa la lie.

Now the inside of this ram, sir,
   Would hold ten sacks of corn,
And you could turn a coach and six
   On the inside of his horn.
Now the wool upon his back, sir,
   It reached up to the sky,
And in it was a crow's nest,
   For I heard the young ones cry.
     That's a lie, that's a lie,
     That's a tid i fa la lie.

ARIEL'S SONG

Full fathom five thy father lies;
   Of his bones are coral made;
Those are pearls that were his eyes:
   Nothing of him that doth fade,
But doth suffer a sea-change
Into something rich and strange:
Sea nymphs hourly ring his knell.
     Ding-dong!
Hark! now I hear them,
    Ding-dong, bell!

WILLIAM SHAKESPEARE

Now the butcher that killed the ram, sir,
   Was up to his knees in blood,
And the boy that held the bowl, sir,
   Got washed away in the flood.
Now all the boys in Derby, sir,
   Went begging for his eyes,
They kicked them up and down the street,
   For they were a good football size.
     That's a lie, that's a lie,
     That's a tid i fa la lie.

Now all the women of Derby, sir,
   Went begging for his ears,
To make their leather aprons of
   That lasted them forty years.
And the man that fatted the ram, sir,
   He must be very rich,
And the man that sung this song, sir,
   Is a lying son of a bitch.
     That's the truth, that's the truth,
     That's the tid i fa la truth.

TRADITIONAL

THE SONG OF THE MAD PRINCE

Who said, 'Peacock Pie'?
   The old King to the sparrow:
Who said, 'Crops are ripe'?
   Rust to the harrow:
Who said, 'Where sleeps she now?
   Where rests she now her head,
Bathed in eve's loveliness'? –
   That's what I said.

Who said, 'Ay, mum's the word';
   Sexton to willow:
Who said, 'Green dusk for dreams,
   Moss for a pillow'?
Who said, 'All Time's delight
   Hath she for narrow bed;
Life's troubled bubble broken'? –
   That's what I said.

WALTER DE LA MARE

FIGGIE HOBBIN

Nightingales' tongues, your majesty?
    Quails in aspic, cost a purse of money?
Oysters from the deep, raving sea?
    Grapes and Greek honey?
Beads of black caviare from the Caspian?
    Rock melon with corn on the cob in?
Take it all away! grumbled the old King of Cornwall.
    Bring me some figgie hobbin!

Devilled lobster, your majesty?
    Scots kail brose or broth?
Grilled mackerel with gooseberry sauce?
    Cider ice that melts in your mouth?
Pears filled with nut and date salad?
    Christmas pudding with a tanner or a bob in?
Take it all away! groused the old King of Cornwall.
    Bring me some figgie hobbin!

Amber jelly, your majesty?
    Passion fruit flummery?
Pineapple sherbet, milk punch or Pavlova cake,
    Sugary, summery?
Carpet-bag steak, blueberry grunt, cinnamon crescents?
    Spaghetti as fine as the thread on a bobbin?
Take it all away! grizzled the old King of Cornwall.
    Bring me some figgie hobbin!

So in from the kitchen came figgie hobbin,
    Shining and speckled with raisins sweet,
And though on the King of Cornwall's land
    The rain it fell and the wind it beat,
As soon as a forkful of figgie hobbin
    Up to his lips he drew,
Over the palace a pure sun shone
    And the sky was blue.
THAT'S what I wanted! he smiled, his face
    Now as bright as the breast of the robin.
To cure the sickness of the heart, ah —
    Bring me some figgie hobbin!

CHARLES CAUSLEY

CALICO PIE

Calico Pie,
    The little Birds fly
Down to the calico tree,
    Their wings were blue,
    And they sang 'Tilly-loo!'
    Till away they flew —
And they never came back to me!
    They never came back!
    They never came back!
They never came back to me!

Calico Jam,
    The little Fish swam
Over the syllabub sea,
    He took off his hat,
    To the Sole and the Sprat,
    And the Willeby-wat —
But he never came back to me!
    He never came back!
    He never came back!
He never came back to me!

Calico Ban,
    The little Mice ran,
To be ready in time for tea,
    Flippity flup,
    They drank it all up,
    And danced in the cup —
But they never came back to me!
    They never came back!
    They never came back!
They never came back to me!

Calico Drum,
    The Grasshoppers come,
The Butterfly, Beetle, and Bee,
    Over the ground,
    Around and round,
    With a hop and a bound —
But they never came back!
    They never came back!
    They never came back!
They never came back to me!

EDWARD LEAR

HOW TO MAKE A SAILOR'S PIE

'Tell me, pray, if you may, how to make a sailor's pie?
First, then, you must take a teacup full of sky!
A strand of hemp, a silent star
And the wind's lullaby,
A flake of foam, a scent of night
And a gull's cry;
A taste of salt, a touch of tar
And a sorrowful goodbye:
Mix all these together, to make a sailor's pie.'

JOAN AIKEN

GREY GOOSE AND GANDER

Grey goose and gander,
Weft your wings together,
And carry the King's fair daughter
Over the one-strand river.

TRADITIONAL

SEA-MARGE

Pebbles are beneath, but we stand softly
On them, as on sand, and watch the lacy edge
Of the swift sea

Which patterns and with glorious music the
Sands and round stones. It talks ever
Of new patterns.

And by the cliff-edge, there, the oakwood throws
A shadow deeper to watch what new thing
Happens at the marge.

IVOR GURNEY

'FERRY ME ACROSS THE WATER'

'Ferry me across the water,
   Do, boatman, do.'
'If you've a penny in your purse
   I'll ferry you.'

'I have a penny in my purse,
   And my eyes are blue;
So ferry me across the water,
   Do, boatman, do.'

'Step into my ferry-boat,
   Be they black or blue,
And for the penny in your purse
   I'll ferry you.'

CHRISTINA ROSSETTI

THE SILVER PENNY

'Sailorman, I'll give to you
   My bright silver penny,
If out to sea you'll sail me
   And my dear sister Jenny.'

'Get in, young sir, I'll sail ye
   And your dear sister Jenny,
But pay she shall her golden locks
   Instead of your penny.'

They sail away, they sail away,
   O fierce the winds blew!
The foam flew in clouds
   And dark the night grew!

And all the green sea-water
   Climbed steep into the boat:
Back to the shore again
   Sail they will not.

Drowned is the sailorman,
   Drowned is sweet Jenny,
And drowned in the deep sea
   A bright silver penny.

WALTER DE LA MARE

'I HAD A LITTLE NUT-TREE'

I had a little nut-tree,
   Nothing would it bear
But a silver nutmeg
   And a golden pear.

The King of Spain's daughter
   Came to visit me,
All for the sake
   Of my little nut-tree.

I skipped over ocean,
   I danced over sea;
And all the birds in the air
   Couldn't catch me!

TRADITIONAL

'INTO MY HEART AN AIR THAT KILLS'

Into my heart an air that kills
   From yon far country blows:
What are those blue remembered hills,
   What spires, what farms are those?

That is the land of lost content,
   I see it shining plain,
The happy highways where I went
   And cannot come again.

A. E. HOUSMAN

THE OWL AND THE PUSSY-CAT

The Owl and the Pussy-cat went to sea
   In a beautiful pea-green boat,
They took some honey, and plenty of money,
   Wrapped up in a five-pound note.
The Owl looked up to the stars above,
   And sang to a small guitar,
'O lovely Pussy! O Pussy, my love,
   What a beautiful Pussy you are,
      You are,
      You are!
   What a beautiful Pussy you are!'

Pussy said to the Owl, 'You elegant fowl!
   How charmingly sweet you sing!
O let us be married! too long we have tarried:
   But what shall we do for a ring?'
They sailed away, for a year and a day,
   To the land where the Bong-tree grows,
And there in a wood a Piggy-wig stood
   With a ring at the end of his nose,
      His nose,
      His nose,
   With a ring at the end of his nose.

'Dear Pig, are you willing to sell for one shilling
   Your ring?' Said the Piggy, 'I will.'
So they took it away, and were married next day
   By the Turkey who lives on the hill.
They dined on mince, and slices of quince,
   Which they ate with a runcible spoon;
And hand in hand, on the edge of the sand,
   They danced by the light of the moon,
      The moon,
      The moon,
   They danced by the light of the moon.

EDWARD LEAR

SPELLS

I dance and dance without any feet –
This is the spell of the ripening wheat.

With never a tongue I've a tale to tell –
This is the meadow-grasses' spell.

I give you health without any fee –
This is the spell of the apple-tree.

I rhyme and riddle without any book –
This is the spell of the bubbling brook.

Without any legs I run for ever –
This is the spell of the mighty river.

I fall for ever and not at all –
This is the spell of the waterfall.

Without a voice I roar aloud –
This is the spell of the thunder-cloud.

No button or seam has my white coat –
This is the spell of the leaping goat.

I can cheat strangers with never a word –
This is the spell of the cuckoo-bird.

We have tongues in plenty but speak no names –
This is the spell of the fiery flames.

The creaking door has a spell to riddle –
I play a tune without any fiddle.

JAMES REEVES

'LEAN OUT OF THE WINDOW'

Lean out of the window,
  Goldenhair,
I heard you singing
  A merry air.

My book is closed,
  I read no more,
Watching the fire dance
  On the floor.

I have left my book:
  I have left my room:
For I heard you singing
  Through the gloom,

Singing and singing
  A merry air.
Lean out of the window,
  Goldenhair.

JAMES JOYCE

'I GIVE YOU THE END
OF A GOLDEN STRING'

I give you the end of a golden string,
  Only wind it into a ball,
It will lead you in at Heaven's gate
  Built in Jerusalem's wall.

WILLIAM BLAKE

GOODNIGHT

GOOD NIGHT

Now good-night.
Fold up your clothes
As you were taught,
Fold your two hands,
Fold up your thought;
Day is the plough-land,
Night is the stream,
Day is for doing
And night is for dream.
Now good-night.

ELEANOR FARJEON

A LYKE-WAKE DIRGE

This ae nighte, this ae nighte,
　Every night and alle;
Fire and fleet, and candle lighte,
　And Christe receive thy saule.

When thou from hence away are paste,
　Every night and alle;
To Whinny-muir thou comest at laste;
　And Christe receive thy saule.

If ever thou gavest hosen and shoon,
　Every night and alle;
Sit thee down, and put them on;
　And Christe receive thy saule.

If hosen and shoon thou ne'er gavest nane,
　Every night and alle;
The whinnies shall pricke thee to the bare bane;
　And Christe receive thy saule.

From Whinny-muir when thou mayst passe,
　Every night and alle;
To Brigg o' Dread thou comest at laste;
　And Christe receive thy saule.

From Brigg o' Dread when thou mayst passe,
　Every night and alle;
To purgatory fire thou comest at laste;
　And Christe receive thy saule.

If ever thou gavest meat or drink,
　Every night and alle;
The fire shall never make thee shrinke;
　And Christe receive thy saule.

If meate or drinke thou never gavest nane,
　Every night and alle;
The fire will burn thee to the bare bane;
　And Christe receive thy saule.

This ae nighte, this ae nighte,
　Every night and alle;
Fire and fleet, and candle lighte,
　And Christe receive thy saule.

TRADITIONAL

Lyke-wake dirge: a song sung at funerals
fleet: water
hosen and shoon: stockings and shoes

A NIGHTMARE

When you're lying awake with a dismal headache, and repose is
    taboo'd by anxiety,
I conceive you may use any language you choose to indulge in without
    impropriety;
For your brain is on fire – the bedclothes conspire of usual slumber to
    plunder you:
First your counterpane goes and uncovers your toes, and your sheet
    slips demurely from under you;
Then the blanketing tickles – you feel like mixed pickles, so terribly
    sharp is the pricking,
And you're hot, and you're cross, and you tumble and toss till there's
    nothing 'twixt you and the ticking.
Then the bedclothes all creep to the ground in a heap, and you pick
    'em all up in a tangle;
Next your pillow resigns and politely declines to remain at its usual
    angle!
Well, you get some repose in the form of a doze, with hot eyeballs and
    head ever aching,
But your slumbering teems with such horrible dreams that you'd very
    much better be waking;
For you dream you are crossing the Channel, and tossing about in a
    steamer from Harwich,
Which is something between a large bathing-machine and a very small
    second-class carriage;
And you're giving a treat (penny ice and cold meat) to a party of
    friends and relations –
They're a ravenous horde – and they all came on board at Sloane
    Square and South Kensington Stations.
And bound on that journey you find your attorney (who started that
    morning from Devon);
He's a bit undersized, and you don't feel surprised when he tells you
    he's only eleven.

Well, you're driving like mad with this singular lad (by the bye the
    ship's now a four-wheeler),
And you're playing round games, and he calls you bad names when you
    tell him that 'ties pay the dealer';
But this you can't stand, so you throw up your hand, and you find
    you're as cold as an icicle,
In your shirt and your socks (the black silk with gold clocks), crossing
    Salisbury Plain on a bicycle:
And he and the crew are on bicycles too – which they've somehow or
    other invested in –
And he's telling the tars all the particulars of a company he's interested
    in –
It's a scheme of devices, to get at low prices, all goods from cough
    mixtures to cables
(Which tickled the sailors) by treating retailers, as though they were all
    vegetables –
You get a good spadesman to plant a small tradesman (first take off his
    boots with a boot-tree),
And his legs will take root, and his fingers will shoot, and they'll
    blossom and bud like a fruit-tree –
From the greengrocer tree you get grapes and green pea, cauliflower,
    pineapple, and cranberries,
While the pastry-cook plant cherry-brandy will grant – apple puffs, and
    three-corners, and banberries –
The shares are a penny, and ever so many are taken by ROTHSCHILD
    and BARING,
And just as a few are allotted to you, you awake with a shudder
    despairing –
You're a regular wreck, with a crick in your neck, and no wonder you
    snore, for your head's on the floor, and you've needles and pins from
    your soles to your shins, and your flesh is a-creep, for your left
    leg's asleep, and you've cramp in your toes, and a fly on your nose,
    and some fluff in your lung, and a feverish tongue, and a thirst that's
    intense, and a general sense that you haven't been sleeping in clover;
But the darkness has passed, and it's daylight at last, and and the night
    has been long – ditto, ditto my song – and thank goodness they're
    both of them over!

        W. S. GILBERT

THE SEA

The sea is a hungry dog,
Giant and grey.
He rolls on the beach all day.
With his clashing teeth and shaggy jaws
Hour upon hour he gnaws
The rumbling, tumbling stones,
And 'Bones, bones, bones, bones!'
The giant sea-dog moans,
Licking his greasy paws.

And when the night wind roars
And the moon rocks in the stormy cloud,
He bounds to his feet and snuffs and sniffs,
Shaking his wet sides over the cliffs,
And howls and hollos long and loud.

But on quiet days in May or June,
When even the grasses on the dune
Play no more their reedy tune,
With his head between his paws
He lies on the sandy shores,
So quiet, so quiet, he scarcely snores.

JAMES REEVES

SLOWLY

Slowly the tide creeps up the sand,
Slowly the shadows cross the land.
Slowly the cart-horse pulls his mile,
Slowly the old man mounts the stile.

Slowly the hands move round the clock,
Slowly the dew dries on the dock.
Slow is the snail – but slowest of all
The green moss spreads on the old brick wall.

JAMES REEVES

TWILIGHT TIME
Shoreham, Kent

And now the trembling light
Glimmers behind the little hills, and corn,
Ling'ring as loth to part: yet part thou must
And though than open day far pleasing more
(Ere yet the fields, and pearled cups of flowers
   Twinkle in the parting light;)
Thee night shall hide, sweet visionary gleam
That softly lookest through the rising dew;
   Till all like silver bright,
   The Faithful Witness, pure, and white,
   Shall look o'er yonder grassy hill,
   At this village, safe and still.
   All is safe and all is still
   Save what noise the watch-dog makes
   Or the shrill cock the silence breaks
      Now and then –
      And now and then –
      Hark! – Once again,
      The wether's bell
      To us doth tell
Some little stirring in the fold.

   Me thinks the ling'ring dying ray
      Of twilight time doth seem more fair
   And lights the soul up more than day,
      When wide-spread sultry sunshines are.
   Yet all is right, and all most fair,
      For Thou, dear God, hast formed all;
   Thou deckest ev'ry little flower,
      Thou girdest ev'ry planet ball –
      And mark'st when sparrows fall.
   Thou pourest out the golden day
   On corn-fields rip'ning in the sun
   Up the side of some great hill
      Ere the sickle has begun.

        SAMUEL PALMER

Samuel Palmer's
COMING FROM EVENING CHURCH

The heaven-reflecting, usual moon
Scarred by thin branches, flows between
The simple sky, its light half-gone,
The evening hills of risen green.
Safely below the mountain crest
A little clench of sheep holds fast.
The lean spire hovers like a mast
Over its hulk of leaves and moss
And those who, locked within a dream,
Make between church and cot their way
Beside the secret-springing stream
That turns towards an unknown sea;
And there is neither night nor day,
Sorrow nor pain, eternally.

CHARLES CAUSLEY

The visionary painter Samuel Palmer (a follower of
William Blake) painted his best work at
Shoreham in Kent. 'Coming from Evening
Church' is in the Tate Gallery, London.

THE ECHOING GREEN

The Sun does arise,
And make happy the skies;
The merry bells ring
To welcome the Spring;
The skylark and thrush,
The birds of the bush,
Sing louder around
To the bells' chearful sound,
While our sports shall be seen
On the Echoing Green.

Old John, with white hair,
Does laugh away care,
Sitting under the oak,
Among the old folk.
They laugh at our play,
And soon they all say:
'Such, such were the joys
'When we all, girls and boys,
'In our youth time were seen
'On the Echoing Green.'

Till the little ones, weary,
No more can be merry;
The sun does descend,
And our sports have an end.
Round the laps of their mothers
Many sisters and brothers,
Like birds in their nest,
Are ready for rest,
And sport no more seen
On the darkening Green.

WILLIAM BLAKE

THE MORNING WATCH

O joys! infinite sweetness! with what flowers
And shoots of glory, my soul breaks and buds!
  All the long hours
  Of night and rest,
  Through the still shrouds
  Of sleep, and clouds,
 This dew fell on my breast;
  O how it bloods,
And spirits all my earth! hark! in what rings,
And hymning circulations the quick world
  Awakes and sings!
  The rising winds
  And falling springs,
  Birds, beasts, all things
 Adore Him in their kinds.
  Thus all is hurl'd
In sacred hymns and order; the great chime
And symphony of Nature. Prayer is
  The world in tune,
  A spirit-voice,
  And vocal joys,
 Whose echo is heaven's bliss.
  O let me climb
When I lie down! The pious soul by night –
Is like a clouded star, whose beams, though said
  To shed their light
  Under some cloud,
  Yet are above,
  And shine and move
 Beyond that misty shroud;
  So in my bed,
That curtain'd grave, though sleep, like ashes, hide
My lamp and life, both shall in Thee abide.

    HENRY VAUGHAN

THE SHEPHERD BOY'S SONG

He that is down, needs fear no fall,
    He that is low, no pride;
He that is humble, ever shall
    Have God to be his guide.

I am content with what I have,
    Little be it, or much:
And, Lord, contentment still I crave,
    Because thou savest such.

Fullness to such a burden is
    That go on pilgrimage:
Here little, and hereafter bliss
    Is best from age to age.

JOHN BUNYAN

THE TIDE IN THE RIVER

The tide in the river,
The tide in the river,
The tide in the river runs deep,
    I saw a shiver
    Pass over the river
As the tide turned in its sleep.

ELEANOR FARJEON

THE SONGS I HAD

The songs I had are withered
Or vanished clean,
Yet there are bright tracks
Where I have been,

And there grow flowers
For others' delight.
Think well, O singer,
Soon comes night.

IVOR GURNEY

A VISION

I lost the love of heaven above
I spurned the lust of earth below
I felt the sweets of fancied love
And hell itself my only foe

I lost earth's joys but felt the glow
Of heaven's flame abound in me
Till loveliness and I did grow
The bard of immortality

I loved but woman fell away
I hid me from her faded fame
I snatched the sun's eternal ray
And wrote till earth was but a name

In every language upon earth
On every shore, o'er every sea,
I gave my name immortal birth,
And kept my spirit with the free

JOHN CLARE

SEA-FEVER

I must down to the seas again, to the lonely sea and the sky,
And all I ask is a tall ship and a star to steer her by,
And the wheel's kick and the wind's song and the white sail's shaking,
And a grey mist on the sea's face and a grey dawn breaking.

I must down to the seas again, for the call of the running tide
Is a wild call and a clear call that may not be denied;
And all I ask is a windy day with the white clouds flying,
And the flung spray and the blown spume, and the sea-gulls crying.

I must down to the seas again, to the vagrant gypsy life,
To the gull's way and the whale's way where the wind's like a whetted knife;
And all I ask is a merry yarn from a laughing fellow-rover,
And quiet sleep and a sweet dream when the long trick's over.

JOHN MASEFIELD

UP-HILL

Does the road wind up-hill all the way?
    Yes, to the very end.
Will the day's journey take the whole long day?
    From morn to night, my friend.

But is there for the night a resting-place?
    A roof for when the slow dark hours begin.
May not the darkness hide it from my face?
    You cannot miss that inn.

Shall I meet other wayfarers at night?
    Those who have gone before.
Then must I knock, or call when just in sight?
    They will not keep you standing at that door.

Shall I find comfort, travel-sore and weak?
    Of labour you shall find the sum.
Will there be beds for me and all who seek?
    Yea, beds for all who come.

CHRISTINA ROSSETTI

REQUIEM

Under the wide and starry sky
Dig the grave and let me lie:
Glad did I live and gladly die,
    And I laid me down with a will.

This be the verse you grave for me
Here he lies where he longed to be;
Home is the sailor, home from sea,
    And the hunter home from the hill.

R. L. STEVENSON

A BABY-SERMON

The lightning and thunder
    They go and they come;
But the stars and the stillness
    Are always at home.

GEORGE MACDONALD

LINES FOR A BED AT KELMSCOTT MANOR

The wind's on the wold
And the night is a-cold,
And Thames runs chill
'Twixt mead and hill,
But kind and dear
Is the old house here,
And my heart is warm
Midst winter's harm.
Rest then and rest,
And think of the best
'Twixt summer and spring
When all birds sing
In the town of the tree,
And ye lie in me
And scarce dare move

Lest earth and its love
Should fade away
Ere the full of the day.

I am old and have seen
Many things that have been,
Both grief and peace,
And wane and increase.
No tale I tell
Of ill or well,
But this I say,
Night treadeth on day,
And for worst and best
Right good is rest.

WILLIAM MORRIS

*These lines were woven into a bed-hanging which can
still be seen at the poet's former home at
Kelmscott in Oxfordshire, England.*

TIME TO GO HOME

Time to go home!
   Says the great steeple clock.
Time to go home!
   Says the gold weathercock.
Down sinks the sun
   In the valley to sleep;
Lost are the orchards
   In blue shadows deep.
Soft falls the dew
   On cornfield and grass;
Through the dark trees
   The evening airs pass:
Time to go home,
   They murmur and say;
Birds to their homes
   Have all flown away.
Nothing shines now
   But the gold weathercock.
Time to go home!
   Says the great steeple clock.

JAMES REEVES

A NIGHT-HERDING SONG

Oh, slow up, dogies, quit your roving round,
You have wandered and tramped all over the ground;
Oh, graze along, dogies, and feed kinda slow,
And don't forever be on the go, –
Oh, move slow, dogies, move slow.

Hi-oo, hi-oo, oo-oo.

I have circle-herded, trail-herded, night-herded, and cross-herded, too,
But to keep you together, that's what I can't do;
My horse is leg-weary and I'm awful tired,
But if I let you get away I'm sure to be fired, –
Bunch up, little dogies, bunch up.

Hi-oo, hi-oo, oo-oo.

Oh say, little dogies, when you goin' to lay down
And quit this forever shiftin' around?
My limbs are weary, my seat is sore;
Oh, lay down, dogies, like you've laid before, –
Lay down, little dogies, lay down.

Hi-oo, hi-oo, oo-oo.

Oh, lay still, dogies, since you've laid down,
Stretch away out on the big open ground;
Snore loud, little dogies, and drown the wild sound
That will all go away when the day rolls round, –
Lay still, little dogies, lay still.

Hi-oo, hi-oo, oo-oo.

HARRY STEPHENS

Harry Stephens was a genuine cowboy of the American West.
'Dogies' was the cowboys' name for their cattle.

THE COTTAGER TO HER INFANT

The days are cold, the nights are long,
The North wind sings a doleful song;
Then hush again upon my breast;
All merry things are now at rest,
  Save thee, my pretty love!

The kitten sleeps upon the hearth,
The crickets long have ceased their mirth;
There's nothing stirring in the house

Save one wee, hungry, nibbling mouse,
  Then why so busy thou?
Nay! start not at the sparkling light;
'Tis but the moon that shines so bright
  On the window-pane
  Bedropped with rain:
Then, little darling! sleep again,
  And wake when it is day.

DOROTHY WORDSWORTH

WEEP YOU NO MORE, SAD FOUNTAINS

Weep you no more, sad fountains;
  What need you flow so fast?
Look how the snowy mountains
  Heaven's sun doth gently waste.
    But my sun's heavenly eyes
    View not your weeping,
    That now lies sleeping
   Softly, now softly lies
    Sleeping.

Sleep is a reconciling,
  A rest that peace begets.
Doth not the sun rise smiling
  When fair at ev'n he sets?
    Rest you then, rest, sad eyes,
    Melt not in weeping
    While she lies sleeping
   Softly, now softly lies
    Sleeping.

ANONYMOUS

SEPHESTIA'S SONG

Weep not, my wanton, smile upon my knee;
When thou art old there's grief enough for thee.
    Mother's wag, pretty boy,
    Father's sorrow, father's joy.
    When thy father first did see
    Such a boy by him and me,
    He was glad, I was woe:
    Fortune changèd made him so,
    When he left his pretty boy,
    Last his sorrow, first his joy.

Weep not, my wanton, smile upon my knee;
When thou art old there's grief enough for thee.
    Streaming tears that never stint,
    Like pearl drops from a flint,
    Fell by course from his eyes,
    That one another's place supplies:
    Thus he grieved in every part,
    Tears of blood fell from his heart,
    When he left his pretty boy,
    Father's sorrow, father's joy.

Weep not my wanton, smile upon my knee;
When thou art old there's grief enough for thee.
    The wanton smiled, father wept;
    Mother cried, baby leapt;
    More he crowed, more we cried;
    Nature could not sorrow hide.
    He must go, he must kiss
    Child and mother, baby bliss;
    For he left his pretty boy,
    Father's sorrow, father's joy.
Weep not, my wanton, smile upon my knee;
When thou art old there's grief enough for thee.

ROBERT GREENE

MY PAPA'S WALTZ

The whiskey on your breath
Could make a small boy dizzy;
But I hung on like death:
Such waltzing was not easy.

We romped until the pans
Slid from the kitchen shelf;
My mother's countenance
Could not unfrown itself.

The hand that held my wrist
Was battered on one knuckle;
At every step you missed
My right ear scraped a buckle.

You beat time on my head
With a palm caked hard by dirt,
Then waltzed me off to bed
Still clinging to your shirt.

THEODORE ROETHKE

GRAMPA

Look him. As quiet as a July river-
bed, asleep, an trim' down like a tree.
Jesus! I never know the Lord could
squeeze so dry. When I was four
foot small I used to say
Grampa, how come you t'in so?
an him tell me, is so I stay
me chile, is so I stay
laughing, an fine
emptying on me –

laughing? It running from him
like a flood, that old molasses
man. Lord, how I never see?
I never know a man could sweet so, cool
as rain; same way him laugh,
I cry now. Wash him. Lay him out.

I know the earth going burn
all him limb dem
as smooth as bone,
clean as a tree under the river
skin, an gather us
beside that distant Shore
bright as a river stone.

DENNIS SCOTT

THE CITY OF SLEEP

Over the edge of the purple down,
    Where the single lamplight gleams,
Know ye the road to the Merciful Town
    That is hard by the Sea of Dreams –
Where the poor may lay their wrongs away,
    And the sick may forget to weep?
But we – pity us! Oh, pity us!
    We wakeful: ah, pity us! –
We must go back with Policeman Day –
    Back from the City of Sleep!

Weary they turn from the scroll and crown,
    Fetter and prayer and plough –
They that go up to the Merciful Town,
    For her gates are closing now.
It is their right in the Baths of Night
    Body and soul to steep,
But we – pity us! ah, pity us!
    We wakeful; oh, pity us! –
We must go back with Policeman Day –
    Back from the City of Sleep!

Over the edge of the purple down,
    Ere the tender dreams begin,
Look – we may look – at the Merciful Town,
    But we may not enter in!
Outcasts all, from her guarded wall
    Back to our watch we creep:
We – pity us! ah, pity us!
    We wakeful; ah, pity us! –
We that go back with Policeman Day –
    Back from the City of Sleep!

RUDYARD KIPLING

AFTER APPLE-PICKING

My long two-pointed ladder's sticking through a tree
Toward heaven still,
And there's a barrel that I didn't fill
Beside it, and there may be two or three
Apples I didn't pick upon some bough.
But I am done with apple-picking now.
Essence of winter sleep is on the night,
The scent of apples: I am drowsing off.
I cannot rub the strangeness from my sight
I got from looking through a pane of glass
I skimmed this morning from the drinking trough
And held against the world of hoary grass.
It melted, and I let it fall and break.
But I was well
Upon my way to sleep before it fell,
And I could tell
What form my dreaming was about to take.
Magnified apples appear and disappear,
Stem end and blossom end,
And every fleck of russet showing clear.
My instep arch not only keeps the ache,
It keeps the pressure of a ladder-round.
I feel the ladder sway as the boughs bend.

And I keep hearing from the cellar bin
The rumbling sound
Of load on load of apples coming in.
For I have had too much
Of apple-picking: I am overtired
Of the great harvest I myself desired.
There were ten thousand thousand fruit to touch,
Cherish in hand, lift down, and not let fall.
For all
That struck the earth,
No matter if not bruised or spiked with stubble,
Went surely to the cider-apple heap
As of no worth.
One can see what will trouble
This sleep of mine, whatever sleep it is.
Were he not gone,
The woodchuck could say whether it's like his
Long sleep, as I describe its coming on,
Or just some human sleep.

ROBERT FROST

PLEASANT SOUNDS

The rustling of leaves under the feet in woods and under hedges;
The crumping of cat-ice and snow down wood-rides, narrow lanes, and every
   street causeway;
Rustling through a wood or rather rushing, while the wind halloos in the
   oak-top like thunder;
The rustle of birds' wings startled from their nests or flying unseen into the
   bushes;
The whizzing of larger birds overhead in a wood, such as crows, puddocks,
   buzzards;
The trample of robins and woodlarks on the brown leaves, and the patter of
   squirrels on the green moss;
The fall of an acorn on the ground, the pattering of nuts on the hazel branches
   as they fall from ripeness;
The flirt of the groundlark's wing from the stubbles – how sweet such pictures
   on dewy mornings, when the dew flashes from its brown feathers!

JOHN CLARE

A SPELL FOR SLEEPING

Sweet william, silverweed, sally-my-handsome.
Dimity darkens the pittering water.
On gloomed lawns wanders a king's daughter.
Curtains are clouding the casement windows.
A moon-glade smurrs the lake with light.
Doves cover the tower with quiet.

Three owls whit-whit in the withies.
Seven fish in a deep pool shimmer.
The princess moves to the spiral stair.

Slowly the sickle moon mounts up.
Frogs hump under moss and mushroom.
The princess climbs to her high hushed room,

Step by step to her shadowed tower.
Water laps the white lake shore.
A ghost opens the princess' door.

Seven fish in the sway of the water.
Six candles for a king's daughter.
Five sighs for a drooping head.
Four ghosts to gentle her bed.
Three owls in the dusk falling.
Two tales to be telling.
One spell for sleeping.

Tamarisk, trefoil, tormentil.
Sleep rolls down from the clouded hill.
A princess dreams of a silver pool.

The moonlight spreads, the soft ferns flitter.
Stilled in a shimmering drift of water,
Seven fish dream of a lost king's daughter.

ALASTAIR REID

'MATTHEW, MARK, LUKE AND JOHN'

Matthew, Mark, Luke, and John,
Bless the bed that I lie on.
Before I lay me down to sleep
I give my soul to Christ to keep.
Four corners to my bed,
Four angels there aspread,
Two to foot, and two to head,
And four to carry me when I'm dead.
I go by sea, I go by land,
The Lord made me with His right hand.
If any danger come to me,
Sweet Jesus Christ deliver me.
He's the branch and I'm the flower,
Pray God send me a happy hour,
And if I die before I wake,
I pray that Christ my soul will take.

TRADITIONAL

A CLEAR MIDNIGHT

This is thy hour O Soul, thy free flight into the wordless,
Away from books, away from art, the day erased, the lesson done,
Thee fully forth emerging, silent, gazing, pondering the themes thou lovest best,
Night, sleep, death and the stars.

WALT WHITMAN

INDEX OF POETS

Aiken, Joan (1924–) 220
Anonymous 56, 208, 242
Arnold, Matthew (1822–88) 195
Auden, W. H. (1907–73) 171

Beaumont, Sir Francis (1584–1616) 204
Bentley, E. C. (1875–1956) 68
Berry, James (1924–) 123, 149
Binyon, Laurence (1869–1943) 150
Bishop, Elizabeth (1911–79) 91
Blake, William (1757–1827) 22, 105, 116, 137, 149, 153, 165, 225, 234
Blishen, Edward (1920–) 211
Brooks, Gwendolyn (1917–) 35
Brown, George Mackay (1921–) 48
Bunyan, John (1628–88) 236
Burns, Robert (1759–96) 22, 62

Callanan, Jeremiah John (1795–1829) 185
Campbell, David (1915–79) 129
Campion, Thomas (1567–1620) 135
Canton, William (1845–1926) 121
Causley, Charles (1917–) 27, 37, 44, 165, 219, 233
Clare, John (1793–1864) 90, 95, 121, 152, 236, 247
Clarke, Gillian (1937–) 25
Clough, Arthur Hugh (1819–61) 163
Coleridge, Samuel Taylor (1772–1834) 94
Collymore, Frank (1893–1980) 63
Cornford, Frances (1886–1960) 73
Cummings, E. E. (1894–1962) 146
Curnow, Allen (1911–) 127

Dallas, Ruth (1919–) 109
Davies, W. H. (1871–1940) 109, 142, 158
De la Mare, Walter (1873–1956) 128, 133, 162, 182, 209, 217, 222
De Vere, Edward, Earl of Oxford (1550–1604) 49
Dickinson, Emily (1830–86) 56, 99, 115, 123, 124, 134, 149, 159, 164, 165
Drayton, Michael (1563–1631) 172

Eliot, T. S. (1888–1965) 67, 87
Elizabeth I, Queen (1533–1603) 55

Farjeon, Eleanor (1881–1965) 53, 228, 236
Farjeon, Herbert (1887–1945) 53
Frost, Robert (1874–1963) 72, 136, 158, 247

Gibson, Wilfrid (1878–1962) 99, 171

Gilbert, W. S. (1836–1911) 229
Glover, Denis (1912–80) 184
Goldsmith, Oliver (?1730–74) 89
Graves, Robert (1895–1985) 25, 27, 60, 70, 77, 95, 142, 202
Greene, Robert (1558–92) 243
Gurney, Ivor (1890–1937) 70, 132, 159, 176, 220, 236

Hardy, Thomas (1840–1928) 111, 124
Hart-Smith, William (1911–) 202
Heaney, Seamus (1939–) 69
Heath-Stubbs, John (1918–) 58, 59, 80
Herrick, Robert (1591–1674) 22, 120
Hood, Thomas (1799–1845) 38
Hopkins, Gerard Manley (1844–89) 97, 146, 162
Housman, A. E. (1859–1936) 76, 119, 144, 187, 222
Hughes, Gillian (1937–) 138
Hughes, Langston (1902–67) 156, 164
Hughes, Ted (1930–) 24, 31, 105, 106, 132
Hulme, T. E. (1883–1917) 30, 124
Hunt, Leigh (1784–1859) 92, 151

Joyce, James (1882–1941) 225

Keats, John (1795–1821) 64, 125, 143, 186, 210
Kipling, Rudyard (1865–1936) 54, 114, 147, 174, 183, 199, 245

Lampman, Archibald (1861–99) 122
Landor, Walter Savage (1775–1864) 68
Larkin, Philip (1922–85) 38, 48, 123
Lawrence, D. H. (1885–1930) 100, 103, 162
Lear, Edward (1812–88) 66, 219, 223

MacDiarmid, Hugh (1892–1978) 156
Macdonald, George (1824–1905) 238
McGough, Roger (1937–) 68
McNaughtan, Adam (1935–) 155
MacNeice, Louis (1907–63) 42, 45, 203
Masefield, John (1878–1967) 237
Mew, Charlotte (1869–1928) 29, 71, 116, 117, 118
Morris, William (1834–96) 237
Muir, Edwin (1887–1959) 36
Murray, Les A. (1938–) 177

Nowlan, Alden (1933–) 104
Noyes, Alfred (1880–1959) 178

Palmer, Samuel (1805–81) 232
Peacock, Thomas Love (1785–1866) 170
Plath, Sylvia (1932–63) 23
Poe, Edgar Allan (1809–49) 36, 207
Porter, Peter (1929–) 75

Quarles, Francis (1592–1644) 97

Ralegh, Sir Walter (?1554–1618) 148, 157
Raleigh, Walter (1861–1922) 72
Ransom, John Crowe, (1888–1974) 33
Reeves, James (1909–78) 110, 224, 231, 240
Reid, Alastair (1926–) 248
Ridley, George (1835–64) 61
Robinson, Edwin Arlington (1869–1935) 187
Roethke, Theodore (1908–63) 244
Ross, W. W. E. (1894–1966) 90
Rossetti, Christina (1830–94) 114, 127, 163, 210, 221, 238

Sackville-West, Vita (1892–1962) 30, 126
Salkey, Andrew (1928–) 204
Sanchez, Sonia (1934–) 73
Schwartz, Delmore (1913–66) 28
Scott, Dennis (1939–) 244
Scott, Sir Walter (1771–1832) 192
Shakespeare, William (1564–1616) 217
Shelley, Percy Bysshe (1792–1822) 148
Sitwell, Edith (1887–1964) 89
Skelton, John (?1460–1529) 29
Smart, Christopher (1722–71) 85
Smith, Iain Crichton (1928–) 156
Smith, Stevie (1902–71) 57, 154
Southey, Robert (1774–1843) 168
Southwell, Robert (?1561–95) 118
Stephens, Harry (fl. 1910) 241
Stevenson, Robert Louis (1850–94) 30, 43, 114, 127, 238
Swenson, May (1919–) 35
Swinburne, A. C. (1837–1909) 50, 145

Tennyson, Alfred Lord (1809–92) 98, 160
Thomas, Dylan (1914–53) 40
Thomas, Edward (1878–1917) 17, 134, 136, 143
Traditional 22, 24, 26, 62, 72, 90, 96, 97, 108, 124, 139, 153, 158, 188, 189, 190, 194, 206, 210, 212, 217, 220, 222, 228, 247
Turberville, George (c.1544–c.1597) 84
Turner, W. J. (1889–1946) 207

Vaughan, Henry (1621–95) 235

Whitman, Walt (1819–92) 20, 67, 106, 247

Williams, William Carlos (1883–1963)

Wilmot, John, Earl of Rochester (1647–80) 56

Wolfe, Charles (1791–1823) 175

Wordsworth, Dorothy (1771–1855) 130, 131, 242

Wordsworth, William (1770–1850) 94, 120, 162

Wotton, Sir Henry (1568–1639) 49

Wright, Judith (1915–   ) 214

Wylie, Elinor (1885–1928) 144

Yeats, W. B. (1865–1939) 35, 51, 144, 205

Young, Andrew, (1885–1971) 98, 137

INDEX OF TITLES
AND FIRST LINES

Titles are in *italics*. Where the title and the first line are the same, the first line only is listed.

A cool small evening shrunk to a dog bark and the clank of a bucket 31

A fish dripping 90

A lizard ran out on a rock and looked up, listening 103

A narrow Fellow in the Grass 99

A noiseless patient spider 106

A snake came to my water-trough 100

A thing of beauty is a joy for ever 143

A touch of cold in the Autumn night 124

A white newspaper sky 138

A wild bird filled the morning air 99

A word is dead 149

Abou Ben adhem (may this tribe increase!) 151

Above the Dock 30

Above the quiet dock in midnight 30

Address to a Child during a Boisterous Winter Evening 130

After Apple-picking 246

Afternoon Tea 71

All the bells of heaven may ring 50

Allie, call the birds in 95

Alone 36

Always – I tell you this they learned – 72

Amazing monster! that, for aught I know 92

Amid the derringers I ride 211

An October robin kept 132

And now the trembling light 232

Anger's Freeing Power 154

Another Grace for a Child 22

Answer to a Child's Question 94

Apple blossom 45

Ariel's Song 217

As I came over Windy Gap 51

As I was going through windy gap 129

As I was going to Derby 216

As you came from the holy land 157

Auguries of Innocence 165

Autumn 124

Autumn Fires 114

Baby-Sermon, A 238

Baby-sitting 25

Ballad of Agincourt, The 172

Ballad of an Old Woman 63

Bang Bang Bang 80

Beachcomber 48

Beautiful, The 158

Because I set no snare 99

Beechwoods at Knole 126

Before the beginning of years 145

Behold! wood into bird and bird to wood again 202

Blazing in Gold and quenching in Purple 123

Boomerang 202

Bread and milk for breakfast 114

Broad August burns in milky skies 121

Brothers, The 36

Bull Moose, The 104

'Bunches of grapes,' says Timothy 209

Burial of Sir John Moore at Corunna 175

Calico Pie 219

Cat, The 89

Cataract of Lodore, The 168

Centaur, The 34

Character of a Happy Life, The 49

Child's Laughter, A 50

Children, if you dare to think 142

Christmas Eve, and twelve of the clock 111

Christmas Song 139

Cities and Thrones and Powers 147

City of Sleep, The 245

Clear Midnight, A 249

Cock-Crow 143

Collar-Bone of a Hare, The 35

Come closer yet, my honeysuckle, my sweetheart Jinny 202

Come, dear children, let us away 195

Coming up England by a different line 38

Consumer's Report, A 74

Cottager to her Infant, The 242

Cows 110

Cuckoo Song 114

Cushie Butterfield 61

Cut grass lies frail 123

Daffodils, The 120

Dark brown is the river 30

Dawlish Fair 210

Day-Dreams 121

Days 48

Dear March – Come in – 115

Derby Ram, The 216

Do you ask what the birds say? The Sparrow, the Dove 94

Does the road wind up-hill all the way? 238

Dolphin plunge, fountain play 203

Domus Cadet Arborem 118

Dont-care didn't care 153

Douglas Tragedy, The 190

Down from the purple mist of trees on the mountain 104

Eagle, The 98
Echoing Green, The 234
Eden Rock 44
Eldorado 207
Even such is Time, that takes in trust 148
Even the rainbow has a body 162
Ever since the great planes were murdered
   at the end of the gardens 118

Fair Daffodils, we weep to see 120
Fair stood the wind for France 172
Fantasy of an African Boy 149
Fern Hill 40
Ferry me across the water 221
Figgie Hobbin 218
First there were two of us, then there were
   three of us 128
First Travels of Max 32
Fish 90
Fish, The 91
For I will consider my Cat Jeoffrey 85
Forsaken Merman, The 195
Fowler, The 99
Frankie and Johnny were lovers 189
Frog Prince, The 57
From childhood's hour I have not been 36
From plains that reel to southward,
   dim 122
From the hag and hungry goblin 208
Full fathom five thy father lies 217
Full Moon 30
Full Moon and Little Frieda 31

Gaily bedight 207
Generations 159
Glog-Hole, The 156
Glory be to God for dappled things 146
God bless our good and gracious King 56
Good Night 228
Good people all, of every sort 89
Grace at Kirkudbright 22
Grampa 244
Grey goose and gander 220
Guid-day now, bonnie Robin 96

Half the time they munched the grass, and
   all the time they lay 110
Hang flags in the airs of July 58
Hares at Play 90
He clasps the crag with crooked hands 98
He that is down, needs fear no fall 236
He was a poet he was 68
He who binds to himself a joy 149
He's gone, and all our plans 176
Heat 122
Henry and Mary 27
Henry was a young king 27
Her strong enchantments failing 187
Here a little child I stand 22
Here am I 133

Here comes a lusty wooer 24
Here lies Fred 56
High Hills, The 132
Highwayman, The 178
His kind velvet bonnet 89
History of the Flood, The 80
House Fear 72
How do I love you, beech-trees, in the
   autumn 126
How does the Water 168
How happy is he born and taught 49
How many miles to Babylon? 206
How pleasant to know Mr Lear 66
How to make a sailor's pie 220
How unpleasant to meet Mr Eliot 67
Hunger 150

I am a frog 57
'I am cherry alive', the little girl sang 28
I am sitting in a strange room listening 25
I am the great sun, but you do not see
   me 165
I caught a tremendous fish 91
I celebrate myself, and sing myself 67
I come among the peoples like a
   shadow 150
I dance and dance without any feet 224
I give you the end of a golden string 225
I had a dream three walls stood up wherein
   a raven bird 154
I had a little nut-tree 222
I had a silver penny 37
I have eaten 72
I have no name 22
I hid my love when young while I 152
I imagine this midnight moment's forest 105
I ken a glog-hole 156
I know where I'm going 26
I lost the love of heaven above 236
I met a traveller from an antique land 148
I must go down to the seas again, to the
   lonely sea and the sky 237
I remember, I remember (Hood) 38
I Remember, I Remember (Larkin) 38
I saw a Peacock with a fiery tale 206
I saw the lovely arch 162
I see a bear 24
I shall lie hidden in a hut 144
I strove with none, for none was worth my
   strife 68
i thank You God for most this amazing 146
I think they were about as high 29
I, too, sing America 156
I took one Draught of Life 165
I wandered lonely as a cloud 120
I was angry with my friend 153
I went out to the hazel wood 205
I will arise and go now, and go to
   Innisfree 144
I wish I loved the Human Race 72

I'm a skyscraper wean; I live on the
   nineteenth flair 155
I'm Nobody! Who are you? 56
I's a broken-hearted keelman, and I's over
   head in love 61
I've watched you now a full half-hour 94
If I might alter kind 84
If you wake at midnight, and hear a horse's
   feet 174
Impromptu on Charles II 56
In an envelope marked 164
In that old house of many generations 32
In that drifting rain in the yard the cows
   are as black 109
In the Fields 116
In the gloom of whiteness 134
In the other gardens 114
In this short life 164
Indulge thy smiling scorn, if smiling still 93
Infant Joy 22
Into my heart an air that kills 222
Invocation 203
'Is there anybody there?' said the
   Traveller 182
it is midnight 73

Jeely Piece Song, The 155
John Connu Rider 204
Jubilate Agno 85

King Arthur 210

La Belle Dame Sans Merci 186
Lady, lovely lady 60
Lake Isle of Innisfree, The 144
Land of Whipperginny, The 202
Lass, I've heard tell 171
Last night I watched my brothers play 36
Lavender's blue, dilly dilly: lavender's
   green 26
Lean out of the window 225
Legend 214
Leisure 142
Let me tell you the story of how I
   began 77
Lines for a Bed at Kelmscott Manor 239
*Lines for Cuscuscaraway and Mirza Murad Ali
   Beg* 67
Listeners, The 182
Little trotty wagtail he went in the rain 95
Lizard 103
Look him. As quiet as a July river 244
Looking-Glass, The 54
Lord Randal 188
Lord, when I look at lovely things which
   pass 116
Love set you going like a fat gold watch 23
Love without hope, as when the young
   bird-catcher 70
Loveliest of trees, the cherry now 119

INDEX OF TITLES AND FIRST LINES

Lover Whose Mistress Feared a Mouse . . . The 84
Loving Mad Tom 208
Lyke-Wake Dirge, A 228

Magpies, The 184
Matthew, Mark, Luke and John 249
Merlin and the Gleam 160
Merry Margaret 29
Michael's Song 99
Milking Before Dawn 109
Mirror, The 25
Mirror mirror tell me 25
Monday I found a boot 48
Morning Song 23
Morning Watch, The 235
Morse 177
My father's friend came once to tea 73
My heart leaps up when I behold 162
My long two-pointed ladder's sticking through a tree 246
My Papa's Waltz 244
My young man's a Cornishman 27

Night-Herding Song, A 241
Nightingales' tongues, your majesty? 218
Nightmare, A 229
None is the same as another 156
Not a drum was heard, not a funeral note 175
Now as I was young and easy under the apple boughs 40
Now good-night 228
Now winter nights enlarge 135
Nursery Rhyme of Innocence and Experience 37

O joys! infinite sweetness! with what flowers 235
O many a day have I made good ale in the glen 185
O my Luve's like a red, red rose 62
O thought I! 131
O what can ail thee Knight at arms 186
O where hae ye been, Lord Randal, my son? 188
O, young Lochinvar is come out of the west 192
O young Mariner 160
Oh, slow up, dogies, quit your roving round 241
On His Seventy-Fifth Birthday 68
On Prince Frederick 56
On the Cuckoo 97
On the Death of a Mad Dog 87
Once I was a young horse all in my youthful prime 108
One leg in front of the other 72
Our Ship she lies in Harbour 194
Out of the wood of thoughts that grows by night 143
Out of us all 17

Outlaw of Loch Lene, The 185
Over the heather the wet wind blows 171
Over the edge of the purple down 245
Over the Hill and over the Dale 210
Over the land freckled with snow half-thawed 136
Owl and the Pussy-Cat, The 223
Oxen, The 111
Oyster, The 90
Ozymandias 148

Pebbles are beneath, but we stand softly 220
Personal 164
Pied Beauty 146
Pleasant Sounds 247
Please to remember 133
Please you, excuse me, good five-o'clock people 71
Pods Pop and Grin 123
Poem at Thirty 73
Poem for a Dead Poet 68
Poison Tree, A 153
Poor Old Horse 108
Prophecy 144

Queen Bess was Harry's daughter. Stand forward partners all! 54

Rainbow, rainbow 124
Rainbow, The (de la Mare) 162
Rainbow, The (Lawrence) 162
Rainbow, The (Traditional) 124
Recollection, A 13
Red, Red Rose, A 63
Repeat that, repeat 97
Requiem 238
Richard Cory 187
'Rise up, rise up, now, Lord Douglas,' she says 190
Road Not Taken, The 158
Robin Redbreast's Testament 96
Roman Wall Blues 171
Romance 207
Rum Tum Tugger, The 87
Running to Paradise 51

Sailorman, I'll give to you 222
Saint Francis and the Birds 69
Samuel Palmer's Coming from Evening Church 233
Say not the struggle nought availeth 163
Sea go dark, dark with wind 127
Sea-Fever 237
Sea-Marge 220
Sea, The 231
Season of mists and mellow fruitfulness 125
Sephestia's Song 243
Shade-catchers, The 29
Shake off your heavy trance 204

She was wearing the coral taffeta trousers 30
Sheep 109
Shepherd Boy's Song, The 236
Silver Penny, The 222
Sing me a song of a lad that is gone 43
Slowly 231
Slowly the tide creeps up the sand 231
Smuggler's Song, A 174
Snake 100
Snow 134
Snow Falling 138
Soap Suds 42
Some have meat and cannot eat 22
Song 152
Song About Myself, A 64
Song by an Old Shepherd 137
Song; Lift-Boy 77
Song of Myself 67
Song of the Galley-Slaves 199
Song of the Mad Prince, The 217
Song of Wandering Aengus, The 205
Songs I Had, The 236
Sound the Flute 116
Spell for Sleeping, A 248
Spells 224
Spring 116
Stopping by Woods on a Snowy Evening 136
Storm, The 128
Strong strong sun, in that look 123
Such a peculiar lot 149
Sudden Thaw 137
Sweet william, silverweed, sally-my-handsome 248

Tell it to the locked-up trees 114
'Tell me, pray if you may . . .' 220
Thaw 136
The Art of Biography 68
The birds are gone to bed, the cows are still 90
The blacksmith's boy went out with a rifle 214
The Brain – is wider than the Sky – 159
The child is father to the man 162
The cuckoo is a merry bird 97
The cuckoo's double note 98
The days are cold, the nights are long 242
The first blossom was the best blossom 45
The heaven-reflecting, usual moon 233
The herring loves the merry moonlight 90
The high hills have a bitterness 132
The idle cuckoo, having made a feast 97
The king sent his lady on the first Yule day 212
The laws of God, the laws of man 76
The lightning and the thunder 238
The lopped tree in time may grow again 118
The miles go sliding by 70

The mountain sheep are sweeter 170
The name of the product I tested is *Life* 74
The Owl and the Pussy-cat went to sea 223
The ploughed field and the fallow field 159
The Rum Tum Tugger is a Curious Cat 87
The rustling of leaves under the feet in
    woods and under hedges 247
The sea is a hungry dog 231
The songs I had are withered 236
The summer that I was ten 34
The Sun and Fog contested 124
The Sun does arise 234
The tide in the river 236
The trees are all bare not a leaf to be
    seen 139
The water is wide, I cannot get o'er 62
The whiskey on your breath 244
The wind was a torrent of darkness among
    the gusty trees 178
The wind's on the wold 239
There lays a ship in the harbour 194
There was a child went forth every day 20
There was a naughty Boy 64
There was an old woman who never was
    wed 63
There's a certain Slant of light 134
They are cutting down the great plane-trees
    at the end of the gardens 117
They are waiting for me somewhere beyond
    Eden Rock 44
They shut the road through the woods 183
This ae nighte, this ae nighte 228
This brand of soap has the same smell as
    once in the big 42
This Is Just to Say 72
This is the weather the cuckoo likes 124
This is the Key of the Kingdom 158
This is thy hour O Soul, thy free flight into
    the wordless 249
Thought-Fox, The 105
Three plum buns 210
Three Sonnets . . . 92
Three things there are more beautiful 158
Tide in the River, The 236

Time to go home! 240
To a Butterfly 94
To Autumn 125
To Daffodils 120
To His Love 176
To Mistress Margaret Hussey 29
To see a World in a Grain of Sand 165
Trees Are Down, The 117
Tuckett. Bill Tuckett. Telegraph operator,
    Hall's creek 177
Twilight Time 232
Two roads diverged in a yellow wood 158
Two Wedding Songs 58
Tyger, The 105
Tyger! Tyger! burning bright 105

Under the wide and starry sky 238
Up-hill 238

Vain and Careless 60
Vision. A 236

Walking Song 70
War Song of Dinas Vawr, The 170
Warning to Children 142
Way through the Woods, The 183
We pulled for you when the wind was
    against us and the sails were low 199
We real cool. We 35
Weathers 124
Weep not, my wanton, smile upon my
    knee 243
Weep you no more, sad fountains 242
Were I a king I could command content 49
What are days for? 48
What are heavy? sea-sand and sorrow 163
What is this life if, full of care 142
What time the wheat field tinges rusty
    brown 121
What way does the Wind come? What way
    does he go? 130
Wheat ripening, The 121
When day dawned with unusual light 137

When Francis preached love to the birds 69
When Good King Arthur ruled the
    land 210
When I was fair and young, and favour
    gracèd me 55
When I was but thirteen or so 207
When I was once in Baltimore 109
When John Connu come', he come' wit'
    style 204
When silver snow decks Sylvio's clothes 137
When Tom and Elizabeth took the
    farm 184
When you're lying awake with a dreadful
    headache, and repose is taboo'd by
    anxiety 229
Whenever Richard Cory went down
    town 187
Whenever the moon and stars are set 127
Where Go the Boats? 30
Where lies the land to which the ship
    would go? 164
White in the moon the long road lies 144
Who has seen the wind? 127
Who said, 'Peacock Pie'? 217
Whose woods these are I think I know 136
Wild Iron 157
William I 52
William the First was the first of our
    kings 52
Wiltshire Downs 98
Windy Gap 129
Windy Nights 127
Wishes of an Elderly Man 72
Wishing-Well, The 171
Words 17
Would I could cast a sail on the water 35

Yankee Doodle went to town 22
Yesterday he was nowhere to be found 106
You strange, astonished-looking, angle-
    faced 92
Young Lochinvar 192
Yule Days, The 212

ACKNOWLEDGEMENTS

We are indebted to the copyright holders for permission to reprint certain poems:

Joan Aiken: to the author and Jonathan Cape Ltd andBrandt & Brandt Inc. for 'How to make a sailor's pie' from BRIDLE THE WIND; W. H. Auden: to Faber & Faber Ltd and Random House Inc. for 'Roman Wall Blues' from COLLECTED POEMS, edited by Edward Mendelson, copyright © 1940 and renewed 1968 by W. H. Auden; James Berry: to Oxford University Press for 'Fantasy of an African Boy' from CHAIN OF DAYS, copyright © James Berry, 1985; to Hamish Hamilton Ltd and Harcourt Brace Jovanovich Inc. for 'Pods Pop and Grin' from WHEN I DANCE; Laurence Binyon: to Mrs Nicolete Gray and The Society of Authors on behalf of the Laurence Binyon Estate for 'Hunger' from COLLECTED POEMS OF LAURENCE BINYON: LYRICAL POEMS (Macmillan, 1931); Elizabeth Bishop: to Farrar, Straus & Giroux Inc. for 'The Fish' from THE COMPLETE POEMS, 1927–1979, copyright © 1979, 1983 by Alice Helen Methfessel; Edward Blishen: to the author for 'Amid the derringers I ride', as reprinted in BAKER'S DOZEN, edited by Leon Garfield; Gwendolyn Brooks: to Harper & Row Publishers for 'We Real Cool' from SELECTED POEMS; George Mackay Brown: to The Hogarth Press Ltd for 'Beachcomber' from FISHERMEN WITH PLOUGHS, 1971; David Campbell: to Angus & Robertson Publishers for 'Windy Gap' from SELECTED POEMS, copyright © Judith Anne Campbell, 1978; Charles Causley: to David Higham Associates Ltd for 'Eden Rock' from A FIELD OF VISION, 'My Young Man's A Cornishman', 'Nursery Rhyme of Innocence and Experience' and 'I Am the Great Sun' from COLLECTED POEMS, 1951–1975, and 'Figgie Hobbin' from FIGGIE HOBBIN; John Clare: to Curtis Brown Ltd, London, for 'Hares at Play', 'Little Trotty Wagtail', 'The Wheat Ripening', 'Song', 'A Vision', and 'Pleasant Sounds', copyright © Eric Robinson; Gillian Clarke: to Gomer Press for 'Baby-sitting' from THE SUNDIAL, 1978; Frank Collymore: to Mrs Ellice Collymore for 'Ballad of an Old Woman' from PENGUIN BOOK OF CARIBBEAN VERSE, 1986; Frances Cornford: to Cresset Press for 'A Recollection' from COLLECTED POEMS, 1954; Iain Crichton Smith: to the author for 'None is the same as another' from SELECTED POEMS, 1955–1980; E. E. Cummings: to Grafton Books and Harcourt Brace Jovanovich Inc. for 'i thank You God for most this amazing' from COMPLETE POEMS, 1936–1962; Allen Curnow: to Penguin Books Ltd for 'Wild Iron' from COLLECTED POEMS, 1933–1973; Ruth Dallas: to the author and John McIndoe Printers & Publishers for 'Milking before Dawn' from COLLECTED POEMS (University of Otago Press, 1987); W. H. Davies: to The Executors of the W. H. Davies Estate, Jonathan Cape Ltd, and Wesleyan University Press Inc. for 'Sheep', 'The Beautiful' and 'Leisure' from THE COMPLETE POEMS OF W. H. DAVIES, copyright © 1963 by Jonathan Cape Ltd; Walter de la Mare: to The Literary Trustees of Walter de la Mare and The Society of Authors as their representative for 'The Storm', 'Please to Remember', 'The Rainbow', 'The Listeners', 'Bunches of Grapes', 'The Song of the Mad Prince' and 'The Silver Penny' from COLLECTED RHYMES & VERSES; Emily Dickinson: to Harvard University Press for 'I'm Nobody! Who are you?', 'A narrow Fellow in the Grass', 'Dear March – Come in', 'Blazing in Gold and quenching in Purple', 'The Sun And Fog contested', 'There's a certain Slant of light', 'A word is dead', 'The Brain – is wider than the Sky', 'In this short Life' and 'I took one Draught of Life' from THE POEMS OF EMILY DICKINSON (The Belknap Press of Harvard University, Cambridge, Massachusetts), copyright © 1951, 1955 by the President and Fellows of Harvard College. T. S. Eliot: to Faber & Faber Ltd and Harcourt Brace Jovanovich Inc. for 'The Rum Tum Tugger' from OLD POSSUM'S BOOK OF PRACTICAL CATS, copyright © 1939 by T. S. Eliot and renewed 1967 by Esme Valerie Eliot; to Faber & Faber Ltd and Harcourt Brace Jovanovich Inc. for 'Lines for Cuscuscaraway and Mirza Murad Ali Beg' from COLLECTED POEMS, 1909–1962, copyright © 1936 by Harcourt Brace Jovanovich Inc., copyright © 1964, 1963 by T. S. Eliot. Eleanor Farjeon: to David Higham Associates Ltd for 'Good Night' and 'The Tide in the River' from INVITATION TO A MOUSE: to David Higham Associates Ltd for 'William I' by Eleanor and Herbert Farjeon from KINGS AND QUEENS; Robert Frost: to the Estate of Robert Frost, the editor, Jonathan Cape Ltd, and Henry Holt & Co. for 'Stopping By Woods on a Snowy Evening', 'The Road Not Taken', 'House Fear' and 'After Apple-Picking' from THE POETRY OF ROBERT FROST, edited by Edward Connery Lathem; W. W. Gibson: to Mr Michael Gibson and Macmillan, London and Basingstoke, for 'The Wishing Well' and 'The Fowler' from COLLECTED POEMS, 1905–1925; Denis Glover: to Richards Literary Agency, Auckland, for 'The Magpies' from SELECTED POEMS (Penguin Books); Robert Graves: to A. P. Watt Ltd and Oxford University Press Inc. for 'Henry and Mary', 'Vain and Careless', 'Love without Hope', 'Song: Lift Boy', 'Allie', 'Warning to Children' and 'The Land of Whipperginny' from COLLECTED POEMS, 1975; to A. P. Watt Ltd for 'The Mirror' from POEMS ABRIDGED FOR DOLLS AND PRINCES (Cassell, 1971); Ivor Gurney: to Oxford University Press for 'Walking Song', 'The High Hills', 'Generations', 'Sea-Marge' and 'The Songs I Had' from COLLECTED POEMS OF IVOR GURNEY, edited by P. J. Kavanagh, copyright © Robin Haines, Sole Trustee of the Gurney Estate 1982; William Hart-Smith: to Angus & Robertson Publishers for 'Boomerang' from SELECTED POEMS, 1936–1984, copyright © William Hart-Smith, 1985; Seamus Heaney: to Faber & Faber Ltd for 'Saint Francis and the Birds' from DEATH OF A NATURALIST; John Heath-Stubbs: to David Higham Associates Ltd for 'Two Wedding Songs' and 'The History of the Flood' from COLLECTED POEMS (Carcanet Press); Gillian Hughes: to Routledge & Kegan Paul Ltd for 'Snow Falling' from THOSE FIRST AFFECTIONS, edited by Timothy Rogers; Langston Hughes: to Alfred A. Knopf Inc. for 'I, Too, Sing America', copyright © 1926 by Alfred A. Knopf Inc. and renewed 1954 by Langston Hughes, and 'Personal', copyright © 1947 by Langston Hughes, both from SELECTED POEMS OF LANGSTON HUGHES; Ted Hughes: to Faber & Faber Ltd for 'I See A Bear' from MOON BELLS; to Faber & Faber Ltd and Harper & Row Publishers for 'Full Moon and Little Frieda' from WODWO, copyright © 1962, 1967 by Ted Hughes; to Faber & Faber Ltd and Harper & Row Publishers for 'The Thought-Fox' from THE HAWK IN THE RAIN', copyright © 1957 by Ted Hughes; copyright renewed 1985; to Faber & Faber Ltd and Harper & Row Publishers for 'Yesterday he was nowhere to be found' and 'An October Robin Kept' from WHAT IS THE TRUTH?, copyright © 1984 by Ted Hughes; James Joyce: to The Society of Authors, the Executors of the James Joyce Estate, Jonathan Cape Ltd, and Viking Penguin Inc. for 'Lean out of the window' from CHAMBER MUSIC; Philip Larkin: to The Marvell Press for 'I Remember, I Remember' from THE LESS DECEIVED; to Faber & Faber Ltd and Farrar, Straus & Giroux Inc. for 'Days' and 'Cut Grass' from COLLECTED POEMS, copyright © 1988, 1989 by the Estate of Philip Larkin; D. H. Lawrence: to Viking Penguin Inc. for 'Snake', 'Lizard' and 'The Rainbow' from THE COMPLETE POEMS. Hugh MacDiarmid: to Michael Grieve and Martin Brian & O'Keeffe Ltd for 'The Glog-Hole' from COMPLETE POEMS; Louis MacNeice: to Faber & Faber Ltd for 'Soap Suds', 'Invocation' and 'Apple Blossom' from THE COLLECTED POEMS OF LOUIS MACNEICE; John Masefield: to The Society of Authors as the literary representative of the Estate of John Masefield for 'Sea-Fever' from COLLECTED POEMS; Roger McGough: to Peters Fraser & Dunlop Group Ltd for 'Poem for a Dead Poet' from HOLIDAY ON DEATH ROW (Cape); Adam McNaughtan: to the author for 'The Jeely Piece Song' from NOISE AND SMOKY BREATH; Edwin Muir: to Faber & Faber Ltd and Oxford University Press Inc. for 'The Brothers' from COLLECTED POEMS, copyright © 1960 by Willa Muir; Les Murray: to Angus & Robertson (UK) for 'Morse' from THE PEOPLE'S OTHERWORLD; Alden Nowlan: to New Books, Trumansburg, New York for 'The Bull Moose' from PLAYING THE JESUS GAME; Alfred Noyes: to John Murray (Publishers) Ltd and Harper & Row Publishers for 'The Highwayman' from COLLECTED POEMS; Sylvia Plath: to Olwyn Hughes and Harper & Row Publishers for 'Morning Song' from COLLECTED POEMS (Faber & Faber), copyright © Ted Hughes, 1971, 1981; Peter Porter: to Oxford University Press for 'A Consumer's Report' from COLLECTED POEMS, copyright © Peter Porter, 1983; John Crowe Ransom: to Laurence Pollinger Ltd and Alfred A. Knopf Inc. for 'First Travels of Max' from SELECTED POEMS, Third Edition, Revised and Enlarged, copyright © 1924 by Alfred A. Knopf Inc. and renewed 1952 by John Crowe Ransom; James Reeves: to Laura Cecil and The James Reeves Estate for 'Cows', 'Spells', 'The Sea', 'Slowly' and 'Time to go Home' from THE COMPLETE POEMS FOR CHILDREN (Heinemann) and THE WANDERING MOON AND OTHER POEMS (Puffin Books), copyright © James Reeves; Alastair Reid: to Margaret Hanbury for 'A Spell for Sleeping' from A GOLDEN LAND; Theodore Roethke: to Faber & Faber Ltd and Doubleday, a division of Bantam Doubleday Dell Publishing Group Inc., for 'My Papa's Waltz' from THE COLLECTED POEMS OF THEODORE ROETHKE, copyright © 1942 by Hearst Magazines Inc.; W. W. E. Ross: for 'Fish' from THE PENGUIN BOOK OF CANADIAN VERSE, edited by Ralph Gustafson; Vita Sackville West: to Nigel Nicolson for 'Full Moon' and 'Beechwoods at Knole' from COLLECTED POEMS; Andrew Salkey: to W. H. Allen & Co. for 'John Connu Rider' from AWAY (Allison & Busby); Sonia Sanchez: to Black Scholar Press for 'Poem at Thirty' from I'VE BEEN A WOMAN, 1978; Delmore Schwartz: to Robert Phillips, Literary Executor, Estate of Delmore Schwartz, for 'I Am Cherry Alive' from SUMMER KNOWLEDGE; Dennis Scott: to University of Pittsburgh Press for 'Grampa' from UNCLE TIME, copyright © 1973 by Dennis Scott; Edith Sitwell: to David Higham Associates Ltd for 'The Cat' from COLLECTED POEMS (Macmillan); Stevie Smith: to James MacGibbon and New Directions Publishing Corporation for 'The Frog Prince' and 'Anger's Freeing power' from THE COLLECTED POEMS OF STEVIE SMITH (Penguin Modern Classics), copyright © 1972 by Stevie Smith; May Swenson: to Little, Brown for 'The Centaur' from NEW AND SELECTED THINGS TAKING PLACE, 1978; Dylan Thomas: to David Higham Associates Ltd and New Directions Publishing Corporation for 'Fern Hill' from COLLECTED POEMS, 1934–1952; Traditional: to Coppersongs for 'Christmas Song' from A SONG FOR EVERY SEASON; William Carlos Williams: to Carcanet Press Ltd and New Directions Publishing Corporation for 'This Is Just To Say' from COLLECTED POEMS VOLUME I, 1909–1939, copyright © 1938 by New Directions Publishing Corporation; Judith Wright: to Angus & Robertson Publishers for 'Legend' from COLLECTED POEMS, 1942–1970, copyright © Judith Wright, 1971; Elinor Wylie: to Alfred A. Knopf Inc. for 'Prophecy' from THE COLLECTED POEMS OF ELINOR WYLIE; W. B. Yeats: to Macmillan Publishing Company for 'The Song of Wandering Aengus' from THE POEMS OF W. B. YEATS: A NEW EDITION, edited by Richard J. Finneran (New York: Macmillan, 1983); Andrew Young: to Martin Secker & Warburg Ltd for 'Wiltshire Downs' and 'Sudden Thaw' from COMPLETE POEMS.

Every effort has been made to trace copyright holders. The Albion Press, in care of the publishers, would be interested to hear from any copyright holders not here acknowledged.